1 SAMUEL
2 SAMUEL

James D. Newsome, Jr.

KNOX PREACHING GUIDES
John H. Hayes, Editor

John Knox Press
ATLANTA

For the people of
The Mars Hill Presbyterian Church
Athens, Tennessee
and
The First Presbyterian Church
Paducah, Kentucky
who taught me what I know about preaching.

Library of Congress Cataloging in Publication Data

Newsome, James D., 1931-
  1 Samuel/2 Samuel.

  (Knox preaching guides)
  Bibliography: p.
  1. Bible O.T. Samuel—Commentaries.
2. Bible. O.T. Samuel—Homiletical use.
I. Title. II. Title: First Samuel/Second Samuel.
III. Series.
BS1325.3.N48   1983   222'.407   82-48092
ISBN 0-8042-3211-3

©copyright John Knox Press 1982
10 9 8 7 6 5 4 3 2 1
Printed in the United States of America
John Knox Press
Atlanta, Georgia 30365

Contents

2 SAMUEL

Introduction

The Books of Samuel are not conventional reading. Such a statement may be made with respect to any part of the Bible, of course, a book which by its very nature is set apart from other literary effort. Yet even in the singular universe of biblical literature, Samuel is an uncommonly vivid constellation, one which has compelled the gaze of generations of readers, young and old, Jewish and Christian, for well over two millenia.

The true temperament of this special quality is not always immediately obvious. At one level the inquirer who wanders into these books is often clutched straightway by the string of compelling stories, artfully told, of people in a variety of circumstances. The young Samuel hearing the voice of the Lord in those hushed, inky hours just before the dawn. Heroic David facing the giant Goliath with no more defense than a shepherd's sling, five smooth stones, and an unswerving faith in God. Poor, mad Saul skulking in disguise through the night to attend the witch of Endor's seance. Uriah the Hittite, faithfully going into battle for his king, tragically ignorant that his sovereign has seduced his wife and arranged his murder. The scandalous harem intrigue of David's declining years with its devices of violent crime and armed insurrection.

Few pieces of literature of such brief duration (some 25,000 words in the received Hebrew text, a small fraction of a modern novel) have ever packed so much drama into so few strokes of the pen. That reader may be appreciated who, having been captured by the sheer emotion of the narrative, treasures the stories for their own value and, remembering them always, moves on to other things.

Yet such a reader will have cheated him/herself by going away with only half a loaf. For beyond all of the individual dramas, with their rich evocation of the joys and sadness of life, 1 & 2 Samuel speak to the ultimate questions of God's relationship to the men and women of his creation. This voice is rarely loud. You may read of all those tortured doings during David's latter years (2 Sam 13–20) and find God mentioned only occasionally. And even when the printed page bristles with the name of God, as in the business concerning his punishment of the Philistines for having captured the sacred Ark (1 Sam 5), it is not language about God to which the modern mind easily relates. Yet subtly textured into the rhythm of the comings and goings of Samuel's characters, human and divine, are themes which not only describe our condition before God, but as well, God's response of justice and love. It becomes part of the preacher's task, therefore, to move beyond the simple narrative appeal of these books and to probe the deeper issues of divine judgment and grace.

How the Books of Samuel Were Written

The Books of Samuel, as we know them in modern versions of the Bible, were not originally separate literary entities. Rather, in combination with 1 & 2 Kings, they formed a history of the Hebrew nation from the time of Samuel, the last of the judges, through the periods of the united and divided monarchies, to the collapse of Jerusalem and the beginning of the Babylonian Capitivity early in the sixth century B.C. The Greek speaking Jews of Egypt appear to have been the first to have divided this history into sections, presumably to facilitate the handling of the large, bulky scrolls upon which the text was copied and from which it was read in public worship. In their translation of the OT, the Septuagint, made in the third or second century B.C., they separated this extensive material into sections entitled the First, Second, Third, and Fourth Books of Kingdoms. It was not until the middle of the fifteenth century A.D. that these divisions were incorporated into printed versions of the Hebrew OT, First and Second Kingdoms becoming First and Second Samuel, Third and Fourth Kingdoms appearing as First and Second Kings.

In using the name Samuel to refer to the first two sections of this history, ancient Jewish traditions were invoked which specified either Samuel alone or in concert with others (see 1 Chron. 29:29) as its author. These traditions flourished, of course, in spite of the fact that Samuel dies fairly early in the story (1 Sam. 25:1). Modern scholarship, however, now knows that the composition of this history was a complex enterprise involving many individuals over an extended period of time. Although a great deal of uncertainty yet remains concerning details, the nature and sequence of this composition appear to have been as follows.

The era before the consolidation of the monarchy under David spawned a number of stories about the persons and institutions central to Israel's life at that time. These stories, which were probably at first independent accounts of specific events, were eventually collected into more lengthy and sequential narratives. Beginning as oral remembrances, this material ultimately received written form and, as it was passed from one generation to the next, was frequently shaped in order that it might speak to the needs and concerns of those who read and heard it. The careers of Samuel, Saul, young David, as well as the fortunes of the sacred chest, the Ark of the Covenant, were the subject matter of the most important of these stories. Traces of these various cycles of stories may still be seen in the present form of 1 Samuel as, for example, stories concerning Samuel in 1 Sam 7:2–17; 8:1–22; 10:17–19a; 12:1–25; concerning Saul in 9:1—10:16; 10:19b–27; 11:1–15; concerning young David (some of these, perhaps, continuations of the stories about Saul) in 18:1–30; 19:11–17; 20:1—21:10; and concerning the sacred Ark in chapters 4–6.

In some instances, a given cycle of stories will find a certain unity not only in its consistent concern for its protagonist, but also in a particular ideological principle, such as the strong anti-royalist sentiment of the Samuel stories (see 1 Sam 8:10–18; 10:17–19a).

Some time after the death of David, perhaps during the high days of Solomon's reign, an exceptionally skilled writer undertook the task of drafting an account of those final turbulent years of David's rule and of the sequence of events which led to Solomon's accession to his father's throne. Although the purpose of the "Succession Narrative," as it has been called, has been the focus of lengthy discussion, one frequently advanced reason for its composition is that it was an effort, likely penned by one of the scribes at Solomon's court, to legitimate the rule of his sovereign, two of whose elder brothers had died in the effort to seize the crown. This material, found in 2 Sam 9–1 Kings 2 (with the exception of 2 Sam 21–24), demonstrates a very sophisticated level of reflection and of artistic creativity. The manner in which the unity of the narrative's theme is maintained in the face of a complex interweaving of plot and sub-plot is remarkable for so early an age, and the skillful use of dialogue and the portrayal of character point to an anonymous writer of great genius. Several qualities, including the subtle theological outlook of the "Succession Narrative," an outlook which only occasionally invokes the name of God, but which nevertheless understands the events described to be the working out of the divine will, point to the influence of the Wisdom Tradition. This tradition, of which the books of Job, Proverbs, and Ecclesiastes are important biblical examples, flourished in many places in the ancient Near East during Solomon's lifetime, and the king's close ties with other nations, especially with Egypt, would have provided ample opportunity for Wisdom ideals to have influenced the intellectual and spiritual life of Solomon's court. The "Succession Narrative," with its juxtaposition of historical recitation and refined theological deliberation is thus viewed by many as one of the finest flowerings of ancient Hebrew literature.

The internal evidence of the text of Samuel-Kings points to the period of the great reformation under Judean King Josiah (2 Kings 22–23), which lasted from 621 until that ruler's death in 609 B.C., as the period when these and other sources, such as stories of the judges, court annals, and tales of the prophets (notably Elijah and Elisha), were edited to produce a vast history of the people of God. Beginning with the biblical Book of Joshua and continuing through 2 Kings (with the exception of Ruth), this history sketched the drama of Israel's life in the land of Palestine until the disaster which befell Jerusalem in 587 B.C. when the city collapsed before the might of the Babylonian army. The apparent influence of the Book of Deuteronomy (probably the "book of the law" in 2 Kings 22:8) upon Josiah's reformation and therefore upon the writing of this history has earned for it the scholarly title "Deuteronomistic History." The written contribution of the editor (who may, of course, have been more than a single individual) is sometimes large and the deuteronomistic interpretation of Israel's history is frequently spelled out in detail: namely, that if the king and the people are faithful to God, the nation will flourish; if not, it will suffer (see 2 Kings 18:1–8 and 21:1–15). At other points the editor is content to stand in the background and allow the material, which he has woven together from his sources, to speak for itself. Most of the passages in the Books of Samuel fall into this latter category.

On one or more subsequent occasions, presumably after the Babylonian Capitivity had sharpened the nation's experience of sin and punishment, two of the main themes of the deuteronomistic historians, further editorial shaping was accomplished which reflected the nation's increased spiritual maturity, but which did not alter the basic form the history had received in the days of Josiah.

Theological Themes in Samuel

The Kingdom of God

Very early in the narrative of Samuel a crisis brews. As a result of the Israelites' inability to stem the Philistine menace under the leadership of the aging Samuel, the leaders of the tribes appear before the priest and demand a king in order "that our king may govern us and go out before us and fight our battles" (1 Sam 8:20). Samuel, after consulting the Lord, reluctantly consents, but not before he delivers an extended warning to his people on the evils which may accompany a monarchial form of government (1 Sam 8:1–18). Clearly the immediate focus of Samuel's concern was the ease with which kings become despots, a fact of life which the Hebrews would have recalled from the stories of their ancestors' sufferings in the Egypt of the Pharaohs. But more profound than the threat to their human rights was Samuel's implied warning that any human king, no matter how well intentioned, would sooner or later encroach upon the prerogatives of Israel's only true king, the Lord. Many years earlier this note had been struck by Gideon when, at the height of his powers, he had refused the crown offered him by a grateful people, saying, "I will not rule over you; the Lord will rule over you" (Judg 8:23). The fact that Samuel's warning against possible political tyranny is, in reality, a warning against potential *spiritual* tyranny is illustrated by the two reasons given for his ultimate break with King Saul. In 1 Sam 13 Saul offers sacrifices to the Lord, although he has not been ordained to the priestly office, while in 1 Sam 15 he violates an important principle of the Holy War by which the enemies of the Lord are to be annihilated completely, down to their very possessions (see Deut 20:16–18; Josh 7:1–26). The latter of these two transgressions would be judged by modern standards to be a commendable example of restraint on Saul's part, but in ancient Israel the matter was viewed differently. And so in sorrow and in anger Samuel pronounces Saul unfit to rule because "you have not kept the commandment of the Lord your God" (1 Sam 13:13; see 15:11). In other words, the human king had violated the authority of Israel's one true king, the Lord.

Yet not all of the spokesmen for God in 1 & 2 Samuel agree with the aged priest and judge in the matter of the role of the human king. A notable exception is the prophet Nathan who, in an important declaration, proclaims that the Lord's plans for the establishment of the dynasty of David date at least from the time of David's shepherd days (2 Sam 7:8). What is more, this dynasty will, under David's successors (notably Solomon), prove to be perpetual because the Lord has "established it so" (2 Sam 7:13, 16). In sum, ancient Israel was of two minds over the question of whether the institution of human kingship would violate the old theocracy by which the nation had lived during the days in the wilderness and in Palestine under the judges.

Yet the point to be stressed is that this disagreement highlighted an important underlying principle to which virtually all important parties in 1 & 2 Samuel assent: *The Lord is Israel's true king.* Those who, like Samuel, warned against a human monarchy did so out of the conviction that the Lord's sovereignty would be compromised. Others, like Nathan, saw the strength of the human monarchy to lie in the fact that it would be the most effective means of "incarnating" the rule of God. All would have sung together

> The Lord reigns; he is robed in majesty . . . Thy throne is established from of old; thou art from everlasting (Psalm 93:1–2).

The Holiness and Judgment of God

Closely allied to the understanding of the kingship of God in 1 & 2 Samuel is the prominence these books give to the theme of God's holiness. In the view of 1 & 2 Samuel that which is holy is that which is beyond ordinary human life. Holiness is the power resident in God himself which, among other things, distinguishes him from his creation. Because this quality is basically unknowable, given the limited capacity of the human mind, it takes the shape of mystery. And because it cannot be contained or controlled by ordinary men and women, it is an object of fear and terror. Yet beyond the terror it looms as a dynamic of love.

Many of the expressions of God's holiness in 1 & 2 Samuel have to do with persons and material objects which, because of their place in Israel's life, have become holy, as it were, by "extension." The Lord's anointed king is one example, whom David twice refuses to kill because of the sacredness of his office (1 Sam 24:6; 26:11). The Ark of the Covenant is another. It causes havoc among the Philistines when it is captured by them (1 Sam 5), poor Uzzah is struck dead trying to spare the Ark a nasty fall (2 Sam 6:6–11), and David's army carries it for protection into battle against the Ammonites (2 Sam 11:11). There was also a kind of "negative holiness" attached to some persons and objects because of their enmity against Israel's God and his plans for his people. (The technical term for this "negative holiness" is *herem*, often translated "devoted thing" in English Bibles.) This concept helps to explain the fate of the Amalekites in 1 Sam 15 (see Num 21:2–3; Deut 20:16–18).

Admittedly, the picture of God's holiness in 1 & 2 Samuel opens the door to a great deal of human suffering. Moreover, in the minds of many ancient Israelites the concept of God's holiness assumed a form which was often little more than crass superstition (1 Sam 6:19). Yet beyond the violence and the superstition, the teaching of 1 & 2 Samuel concerning God's holiness is an important means by which these books stress God's "otherness," his transcendence and dominion over human life. There is no anthropomorphism in 1 & 2 Samuel, no "Lord God walking in the garden in the cool of the day" (Gen 3:8). God is God and humanity is humanity, and the two do not meet except as God, who loves Israel as his own people, wills it.

God's holiness is also the background out of which 1 & 2 Samuel understand God's judgment. In ancient Israel the connection between God's holiness and his moral passion was made by both priest (Lev 19:2) and prophet (Amos 4:1–3). It is therefore not surprising that 1 & 2 Samuel, which views the holiness of God in such a serious light, should make this connection also. Three of early Israel's prominent families are dismissed from their special responsibilities before God because of their moral unworthiness: Eli (1 Sam 2:27–31), Samuel (8:1–5), and Saul (13:13–14; 15:10–11). And no less a person than great King David himself is challenged by the Lord's prophet Nathan because he caused the death of one of his own soldiers and added the man's wife to the royal harem (2 Sam 12). The death of David's child born of this scandalous union is viewed as the consequence of David's sin (v. 14), but the real force of the narrative lies in its description of Nathan, God's man of the hour, who took the astonishing step of reminding David that the Lord's annointed cannot conduct himself as a cheap despot.

1 & 2 Samuel are written out of the conviction that a holy God is just and righteous in all his ways, and that he therefore demands justice and moral responsibility from his people.

The Mercy of God

Contrary to some popular opinion, the OT rarely speaks of God's judgment without also speaking some corresponding word of God's love. 1 & 2 Samuel are no exception, and in this literature "grace abounds."

God responds to Hannah's prayer for a child by giving her Samuel (1 Sam 1:1–20). Samuel's purity is acknowledged by the Lord who makes of the young man a primary means by which he communicates with his people (1 Sam 3:19–21). The repentance of the nation for its idolatrous ways results in military deliverance (1 Sam 7:3–11). David's contrition over his sin in the matter of Bathsheba and Uriah makes possible the grace by which his own life is saved (2 Sam 12:13). And his repentance over having ordered the census of his people—an act which implied that David was yielding to those despotic temptations graphically described by old Samuel (1 Sam 8:10-18)—softens the Lord's angry response (2 Sam 24:10-17).

The mercy of God is written in larger characters, however, than simply his benevolent response to acts of contrition on the part of individual men and women, or for that matter, his response to the beauty of a life well and faithfully lived. The deuteronomistic historians, who were responsible for the final shape of Samuel-Kings, enthusiastically embraced this view of the manner in which God's grace operates. Yet there was another aspect to their comprehension of God's love and, although their point of view is more transparent in that literature which inspired them, the Book of Deuteronomy, and in the narrative of the Divided Monarchy in 1 & 2 Kings, it may be seen here in 1 & 2 Samuel as well. The larger shape of their vision of God's grace extended to the conviction that, although individuals as well as the nation would either prosper or suffer according to the quality of their commitment to the Lord and his ways, Israel was God's special people and he therefore supported and sustained them quite apart from any superior piety or morality on their part. In other words, God is a benevolent fact in Israel's life whether she deserves him or not.

Again the concept of the holiness of God lies at the heart of the matter. God is holy and his people are holy by "extension."

> For you are a people holy to the Lord your God; the Lord your God has chosen you to be a people for his own possession, out of all the peoples that are on the face of the earth. It was not because you were more in number than any other people that the Lord set his love upon you and chose you, for you were the fewest of all peoples; but it is because the Lord loves you, and is keeping the oath which he swore to your fathers. . . (Deut 7:6-8).

Thus beneath the undulating pattern of sin–punishment–repentance–salvation, so common to the deuteronomistic literature, there is a bedrock of divine benevolence toward Israel which operates in good times and in bad. Saul

may defile the office of the Lord's anointed king, especially in
the eyes of old Samuel, but God's mercy operates to raise up
a greater than Saul. David's lust for Bathsheba eventuates,
by the grace of God, in the birth of his heir Solomon, whose
name will rival that of his father for riches, wisdom and
piety. And the convulsive civil turmoil which mars David's
latter years and which must be regarded as a result of
David's weakness in ordering the life of his own household
(note 1 Kings 1:6), ultimately yields to the most protracted
period of economic and political stability the United Monarchy was to know. Thus, the understanding of 1 & 2 Samuel is
that God's grace operates in the life of his people not only in
response to their moral and spiritual commitment, but frequently in spite of its absence.

The Freedom of Man and Woman

It has been observed by a number of students of the OT
that the period of the United Monarchy was the era which
produced humankind's first efforts in the writing of history
(in the modern sense of that word). One of these was the
work of the Yahwist ("J"), now to be found incorporated into the text of Genesis-Numbers. The other was the Succession Narrative of 2 Sam 9–1 Kings 2 (omitting 2 Sam
21–24). It is not surprising that this latter literature should
contain theological motifs which are distinctive in their emphasis when compared with the remainder of Samuel-
Kings. One of these is the picture of the freedom in which
men and women live.

The reader who moves through the Succession Narrative
from beginning to end will be impressed by its fascination
with individual human personalities and with the sparks
which the interaction of these personalities kindles. Witness
the skillful interweaving into the main thread of the story
(which has to do with the question of who will succeed David
as king) of a number of sub-plots which are concerned with
the fate of specific individuals: the stories about
Mephibosheth (or Meribaal, perhaps his real name—see 1
Chron 8:34), about Joab, and about the people in David's
own household. Witness the artful use of such devices as dialogue between characters and the revelations concerning secret thoughts and private actions of persons in the story.

Witness also the almost complete absence of the direct intervention of God in the drama: there are no miracles, no vi-
sions or dreams, no sudden revelations.

The impact of all of this is to make the reader understand that the events being described are moving along according to a momentum of their own. Actions transpire and
climaxes are achieved (including the final climax: the coronation of Solomon) on the basis of a complex series of
human causes and effects. This does not mean that, for the
author of the Succession Narrative, God is absent or non-
existent, as we will discuss in a moment. It does mean, however, that the men and women of the drama act with enormous freedom.

And the characters themselves conduct their affairs as if
they are aware of this freedom and intend to utilize it fully.
Nathan's freedom in denouncing his sovereign's immorality
and treachery (2 Sam 12) has already been noted. Joab exercises much the same kind of freedom when, following Absalom's death, he admonishes David sternly to remember that
his responsibility is not to dead Absalom, but to his faithful,
living subjects (2 Sam 19:5–7). David's own freedom is exercised when, during his flight from Jerusalem to escape the
army of Absalom, he orders the Ark to be returned to the city,
saying, in effect, that the Lord will save or condemn him on
the basis of his merit and not according to the proximity of
that sacred talisman (2 Sam 15:25—compare the very different attitude of the people in 1 Sam 4:1–4).

Yet the freedom which is so prominent in the Succession
Narrative is not unconditional. It is rather shaped and limited by the God who grants and presides over it. Three texts
emerge, the force of which is that events in the drama take a
certain turn simply because God is present, loving and judg-
ing. "The thing that David had done displeased the Lord" (2
Sam 11:27) sets the stage for Nathan's rebuke. "And [Bath-
sheba] bore a son, and [David] called his name Solomon. And
the Lord loved him" (2 Sam 12:24) points to the final outcome of the drama. "For the Lord had ordained to defeat the
good counsel of Ahithophel so that the Lord might bring evil
upon Absalom" (2 Sam 17:14) signals the coming collapse of
Absalom's tragic rebellion. In other words, in spite of the
freedom which the characters in this drama enjoy, there are

certain limits beyond which they may not venture without serious peril. To acknowledge these limits and to consent to live within them is, for the Succession Narrative, an important expression of faith in God.

The Faith Which Saves

Faith, indeed, is the capstone of the theology of 1 & 2 Samuel. If it is true that the various strata which went into the composition of these books display differences of spiritual emphasis, it is equally true that all of them are agreed that the special relationship which God has initiated with his people demands a certain response from them.

The cycles of stories about Samuel, Saul, and young David, representing the most ancient layers of material, describe this response primarily in terms of trust. They have as a frequent theme the declaration that the God who has brought his people to this point in their pilgrimage will not desert them now, if only they will demonstrate their confidence in his protective love. Because these stories date from a period in which Israel's existence was severely threatened, the expressions of trust which they describe were frequently offered amid the sounds of battle. Thus, Samuel prays and sacrifices to the Lord in the face of a Philistine invasion (1 Sam 7:9–10). Saul acts in a similar manner before the Hebrew military encampment at Gilgal (1 Sam 13:8–14). And the young David, volunteering for combat with Goliath, recounts God's gracious acts of protection in his own shepherd past and affirms: "The Lord who delivered me from the paw of the lion and from the paw of the bear, will deliver me from the hand of this Philistine" (1 Sam 17:37).

The Succession Narrative, as we have seen, breathes the sophisticated enlightenment of the court of Solomon. The wars of the past, including the recent struggles for possession of the throne of David, are now over. The nation is secure within her own borders, her life ordered from above by a monarch whose very name (from the root *shalom*) means "peace." So in this part of our material the response of God's people to his presence in their lives is not described in terms of "prayers from the foxhole" (which is somewhat remarkable in view of the large amount of attention in the Succession Narrative to the movement of troops and the fighting of battles). The response is rather the acknowledgment of God's presence and the confession that the established order represents his will for Israel's life.

As we have just noticed in the preceeding section, the Succession Narrative understands faith, in part at least, as an acceptance of the limits within which life is to be lived. When these limits are breached, the consequences fall not just upon the individual sinner, but upon the whole social order. The rape of Tamar (2 Sam 13) sets in motion a civil war which does not end until Absalom is killed and David's heart is broken. David's ordering of the census (a pericope generally considered outside the body of the Succession Narrative proper, but one which shares with it certain things in common) brings a plague upon all Israel (2 Sam 24:15). And David's foolish indulgence of his son Adonijah (1 Kings 1:6) results in further civil disruption and bloodshed. There can be little doubt that, by painting the terrors of the immediate past in such vivid colors, the author of the Succession Narrative wished to contrast favorably the present stability of the Solomonic kingdom and to elicit from his readers a commitment to the God of order which would assure the continuation of that stability.

The deuteronomistic historians, in their turn, left yet another understanding of faith. Because they drew their inspiration from King Josiah's newly discovered "book of the law" (2 Kings 22:8), that is, the Book of Deuteronomy, it is probably there that we find the most succinct statement of their theology of faith:

> You shall diligently keep the commandments of the Lord your God, and his testimonies, and his statues, which he has commanded you. And you shall do what is right and good in the sight of the Lord... (Deut 6:17–18).

Here, faith is the *doing* of what God commands (for example, the Ten Commandments which shortly precede the above text in Deut 5). But it is also the *incorporation* of the commandments of God into one's heart and life (cf. Deut 4:1; 10:16; 15:9). For the deuteronomistic historians, faith is the internalizing of the law in such a way that it becomes a part of one's own being (notice the similar view of the prophet

Jeremiah, a contemporary of the deuteronomistic historians, in Jer 31:31–34).

Although specific editorial contributions of the deuteronomistic historians are much rarer in Samuel than in Kings, the framework of Samuel reveals their theological concerns. Notably, Saul is doomed, not just because of specific transgressions, as the old stories had it (1 Sam 13; 15), but because of his lack of piety, the absence of a fundamental inclination in his heart toward the Lord. On the other hand, David, in spite of moral blemishes upon his character at least as great as those of Saul, prospers because of the basic "bent" of his soul. Read the section 1 Sam 9–30 and notice how few references may be found concerning Saul's commitment to the Lord, compared with those which describe David's devotion (17:26; 24:6; 26:9). Saul had so distanced himself from the Lord that, when he turns to him in the end, the gulf is too great to bridge (1 Sam 28:6).

In summary, 1 & 2 Samuel describe faith in God as a necessary response to the Lord's presence in Israel's life. The shape of that faith and the manner in which it is expressed reflect the circumstances bearing upon the life of the people at a given moment.

1 SAMUEL

Samuel:
Prophet, Priest, and Judge
(1 Samuel 1:1—7:17)

The first section of 1 Samuel is devoted primarily to a description of the rise to leadership in Israel of Samuel. Structurally, this section also contains a block of material whose primary interest lies in the Ark of the Covenant (chapters 4–6).

The Birth of Samuel (1:1–28)

The background of this passage seems to be the important autumnal festival which the OT Hebrews, like many other peoples in the ancient Near East, celebrated annually. In Israel this was a time of thanksgiving for the harvest of summer crops (primarily grapes and olives) and, on a more somber note, a time of reflection and repentance, as symbolized by the beginning of a New Year (Rosh Hashanah) and the observance of the Day of Atonement (Yom Kippur). During the period of the monarchy it may also have been an occasion, at least in Judah, when the king was ceremonially reenthroned and reaffirmed by the priests of God as the divinely appointed ruler, a practice which we know was common among some of the Hebrews' neighbors. In early Israel, however, the autumn festival was generally a family affair and the annual journey to Shiloh or to some other important shrine was a time of celebration and recommitment to the Lord. It is in this spirit that Elkanah and his household understood their yearly pilgrimage. Therefore, the sadness of Hannah, superimposed upon this warm and familial scene and made all the worse by the needling of fruitful Peninnah, is stark indeed.

The portrait of a barren woman would have aroused deep sympathy among many ancient Hebrews and it appears several times in the Scriptures (see Gen 16; Luke 1). In biblical times one's children were often the only form of Social Security available for old age. In addition, for such a people as the ancient Hebrews, whose vision of life beyond death was vague, or non-existent (see Job 14:10–12), children were a means of perpetuating the family name and, vicariously, one's own personality. And so the story of Hannah, praying in muted desperation before the Lord (vs. 10–11), would have touched the hearts of many in old Israel. That the priest Eli mistook her intensity of spirit for alcoholic intoxication (v. 14) only served to emphasize the distressed nature of her predicament.

Modern readers are not always caught up in the tension of this drama as earlier generations may have been. Current medical techniques are available which are often successful in correcting the causes of infertility and which have helped erect a distance between our world and that of Hannah. Also, while children are still just as loved and cherished (at least in those homes where spiritual and psychic health prevails), they are no longer considered a means of the family's economic survival. Quite the contrary! A large portion of a family's income now goes to feeding, clothing, and educating its offspring—in short, to preparing a younger generation to support the generation which will follow. And so the temptation is to read the plight of Hannah with the benign indulgence which remembers that the world was once a very different kind of place.

However, the electricity in this story does not consist in Hannah's anguish over the condition of her body, at least not primarily. It is generated by that paradox between the barrenness of her womb and the fertility of her spirit (notice the reason Hannah gives for wanting a son, v. 11). In other words, although that which she cherished most in life had been denied her, she had not sloughed off hope, nor had she allowed the gloating of Elkanah's other spouse to embitter her. She seized the occasion of the family's annual pilgrimage to the sanctuary at Shiloh—in this period Israel's most holy place, the home of the Ark of the Covenant—to renew her petition to God. And it is a further evidence of the beauty of this woman that, when her yearning is fulfilled by the birth of the boy Samuel, she forfeits many of those benefits which parenthood was expected to confer by handing the lad over to Eli to be enlisted into the service of God (v. 28). And so the theme of these verses which open the Books of Samuel is not that of simple, frustrated desires, as an unsuspecting reader might at first assume. It is rather that of selfless hopes denied, then fulfilled, a fulfillment which is understood largely on the basis of the trust in God which generated those hopes to begin with.

"Serendipidity is a Four Letter Word." Hope is basic to faith. It is one of the corollaries of faith (1 Cor 13:13) and, in biblical thought, it helps to distinguish true commitment from simple blind trust. The latter, as exercised, for example, by the prophets of Baal (1 Kings 18), is capable of systems of tyranny and despotism (compare Jonestown). Hope, however, resonates to the nature of God as love. It anticipates joy and, ultimately, it is not disappointed.

This does not mean that all dreams come true in precisely the way in which we dream them. "What if" Hannah had remained barren for life? "What if" good Elkanah had proved less sympathetic to her plans to dedicate the lad to the Lord as a Nazirite (v. 11—after all, Samuel was his son too!)? "What if" the lad had rebelled against the role his parents chose for him? No one knows the answers to these questions, of course, for the simple reason that the "what ifs" in life are generally unfathomable.

Yet when we remember that 1 Sam 1 is not only a narrative about Samuel's origin, but primarily an essay dealing with the relationship between faith and hope, we may suppose that Hannah would have found some other outlet for her conviction concerning the basic goodness of God. If a child had continued to be denied to her, she would likely have redoubled her devotion to her husband and, yes, even to the children of her rival Peninnah. Or had Samuel for some reason rejected the role to which he had been consecrated, it is possible that she herself would have increasingly discovered avenues for serving the Lord and meeting the needs of ordinary men and women. (An interesting parallel here is the story of the faith of Monica, the mother of Augustine, in contrast to the early lack of commitment of her son, a parallel which might be extended to say something about the saving effect of parents' faith upon the lives of their children.)

In other words, God has a way of responding to human aspirations which is sometimes quite surprising, a response which often seems related to the way in which we do our hoping. That hope which is parochial and inward, which envisions joy only in terms of its own specific fulfillment, frequently dies when that fulfillment is denied, or worse, turns evil and violent. Yet the hope which looks beyond a finely focused attainment and tries to catch some shape of the larger place of its fulfillment more easily tolerates frustration and more gracefully moves on to alternative forms of fulfillment.

Perhaps the important word which this text delivers is that human hope is the ability of the individual to be faithful to the love of God, when that love is plainly evident and even when it is not.

Hannah's Thanksgiving (2:1–10)

The second chapter of 1 Samuel is a study in opposites. Hannah's song, with its clash of contrasts such as rich-poor, weak-strong, joy-sadness, is the first instance of this.

In reading Hannah's Thanksgiving one is likely to remember the Magnificat, Mary's song of joy over the impending birth of her son (Luke 1:46–55). Many of the same contrasting symbols are set against one another in Mary's song as in Hannah's, and the basic message is repeated: God is a strong advocate of justice, and those sinful values and structures upon which men and women have placed their hopes will eventually be overturned so that what is up will be down, what is in will be out. For Hannah, Samuel is God's pledge that this is the way things will come to pass. For Mary, the same is true of Jesus, except in even more sweeping, fundamental ways.

Much of the attention of both Hannah and Mary is devoted to economic and political inequity. It has probably been true in every human society that wealth has tended to corrupt and degrade. Old Israel certainly had such an experience! The Davidic monarchy which saved the nation from those Philistines who tried to oppress it itself led to such economic exploitation that civil strife erupted. And later, in the Northern Kingdom, the financial prosperity that resulted from that nation's alliance with the rich Phoenician maritime centers of Tyre and Sidon violently polarized society between the monied merchantile and ruling classes, to one side, and the dirt poor peasants, to the other. The story of King Ahab's mistreatment of the farmer Naboth in 1 Kings 21 is a good example of the oppression in those days of the poor by the rich, as the account of Jehu's bloody revolt in 2 Kings 9 is the story of the fierce backlash such oppression evoked. In Jesus' time things seemed little different, the rich patronage of Rome propping up the puppet kings of the Herodian dynasty, so that the murder of the young children in Matt 2:16–18 is by no means unbelievable.

It's little wonder that Hannah looks forward to a day when

Those who were full [will] have hired themselves out for
  bread,
but those who were hungry [will] have ceased to hunger
  (v. 5).

For strikingly similar passages in the NT, read Matt 19:24 and Luke 1:53.

Yet the Scriptures provide an understanding of the nature of economic wealth and the power that usually accompanies it which is complementary to that found in Hannah's poem. The Book of Deuteronomy, for example, which as much as any other literature in the OT projects the moral obligations men and women have before God (even, at one point, to a description of how a forest should be treated in time of war—Deut 20:19–20), talks of material prosperity in positive tones:

Hear therefore [my commandments], O Israel, and
  be careful to do them; that it may go well with you,

and that you may multiply greatly, as the Lord, the God of your fathers, has promised you, in a land flowing with milk and honey (Deut 6:3; see Prov 21:13; 22:16).

And for every Rich Young Ruler who turned away from Jesus because he would not turn away from his treasure (Mark 10:17–22), there may have been a Joseph of Arimathea, not afraid of putting his property and wealth on the line by, in this instance, claiming the body of our Lord for burial in his own sepulchre (Matt 27:57–60).

Perhaps it all comes down to the fact that "God's is a Topsy-Turvy Kingdom." In our town a new ordinance provides that when a landlord fails to pay the utility bill on his rental property (where such an obligation is part of the rental agreement), the landlord's own utilities, not the tenant's, may be disconnected. Hannah and Mary would doubtless approve. Economic prosperity which is generated by honest industry is a gift of God. But like his other gifts, money can be abused or misapplied so that it works to the distress and injury of others. In our time the complex nature of international finance and corporate organization has perhaps increased that danger. Yet understood as an extension of the presence of God himself and used in the spirit of one answerable to the Poor Man of Nazareth who had no pillow for his head, our wealth and the power it generates may become a means of praising God and ennobling the lives of his children. Hannah and Mary both remind us that God will not stand for it to be used in any other way!

The Treachery of Eli's Sons (2:11–36)

The clash of opposites, begun with the contrasting themes of Hannah's Thanksgiving, now continues in this study of the vulgar behavior of Eli's sons. All that is involved in the matter having to do with the sacrifices in vs. 13–17 is not entirely clear. Although Lev 7:28–36, Num 18:8–20, and Deut 18:3 describe how certain parts of an animal sacrifice were to be set aside for the priests, our passage seems to have other ritual provisions in mind. What is clear, however, is that Hophni and Phinehas were greedy and that they were abusing their sacred offices by extorting the choicest parts of the uncooked meat from the worshippers. The shocking charge of illicit sexual relationships (v. 22) may in some manner relate to the practice of cultic prostitution in vogue at certain Canaanite shrines.

As if the final compiler of this story wished to weave a tapestry, the dark fibers of the priests' sacrilege are interrupted at important points by the emerging bright thread of young Samuel's purity and innocence (vs. 18–20, 26). And lying side by side, the two patterns of behavior seem all the more at odds. How could Hophni and Phinehas stoop so low, we are asked to wonder. How could the boy remain so essentially good in such a corrupted atmosphere?

The second brief summary of Samuel's character forcefully anticipates what Luke is later to write about the boy Jesus, a similarity which provides us with another reason (in addition to the close parallels between Hannah's Thanksgiving and Mary's Magnificat) to believe that the author of the Third Gospel had drunk deeply from the story of young Samuel:

> Now the boy Samuel continued to grow both in stature and in favor with the Lord and with men (1 Sam 2:26).
> And Jesus inceased in wisdom and in stature and in favor with God and man (Luke 2:52).

The climax of the narrative is contained in the speech of an anonymous "man of God," probably a seer who, like others of his order, was considered capable of divining the future. The man's point is tragic and unmistakable: Eli's family is to be disqualified from its role as special custodians of Israel's holy traditions and is to be replaced by another family, as yet unnamed. The astonishing thing is that the new family of priests will not belong to Samuel, as the interplay of moral contrasts which lead up to the seer's speech would lead us to suppose, but to a certain Zadok (2 Sam 8:17; 1 Kings 2:27). By that time, however, Samuel will be dead, along with the descendants of Eli, their respective reputations enshrined in the memory of the people of God by this tragic and touching story.

We are handling here more than a simple tale of God's displeasure over the sinful ways of men and women, although that theme is certainly present. Nor is the story spun merely to provide an answer to later generations of Hebrew readers as to "Whatever happened to the old priests of Eli?" That purpose is also intended here. However, the larger theme, to go back to the motif of contrasting opposites, seems to have to do with the desecration of their holy office by the unholy sons of Eli, a sacrilege made all the more blatant because of the contrasting faithfulness to God of young Samuel. The theology of the story is thus summarized by two statements which appear repeatedly in Samuel (in various forms of expression), often in close proximity to one another (see Introduction). (1) The result of human sinfulness is alienation from God, as symbolized here in the condemnation of the house of Eli, and (2) even as God condemns, his grace is active in the effort to save his people, the present evidence of which is the deepening spiritual maturity of Samuel.

Thus, at least two themes emerge here, one of which may be food for thought in connection with the minister's own spiritual formation, the other grist for the preacher's mill. First, is there a sense in which the minister, as the custodian of the holy, is expected to live a morally exemplary life? To one side are those voices which tell us that the minister is, after all, only human and that he/she should not be expected to perform extraordinary feats of morality which are not demanded of others. Indeed, we are reminded, any double standard of conduct imposed upon clergy is a repudiation, at least for Protestants, of the important principle of the priesthood of all believers. Moreover, to expect the minister (and perhaps his/her family) to live upon some moral pedestal is to add a crushing weight to the already heavy psychological stresses which ministers must endure as a consequence of their everyday vocational duties.

Those on the other side of the discussion, however, would suggest that if the Christian ideals for moral conduct cannot find something approaching fulfillment in the lives of those men and women who have responded to God's call to speak his word, how can other Christians find models for their own lives? Or how can that word be believed if in some important manner it does not express itself in the life of him/her who speaks it? In Chaucer's words, "If gold rusts, what will poor iron do?"

However one may feel about the above discussion, the theology of this passage in 1 Sam 2 must be taken into account. It seems clearly to expect certain attitudes and deeds from those who are appointed to "handle" holy things. Because the family of Eli repudiates this responsibility, it stands under the judgment of God. Because Samuel embraces it, God begins more and more to use him (see 1 Sam 3:19–21).

God's use of Samuel is the focus of the second theme, that of God's grace, and perhaps of a sermon entitled "Don't Forget the Pedals!"As a boy I labored over the piano lessons my parents wisely encouraged me to take. After a great deal of effort I was usually able to coordinate my fingers sufficiently to pound out a simple piece at recital time. I was never able to fathom, however, how a close friend managed to play the organ at our church. He not only had banks of keys for his skillful fingers to manipulate, but his *feet* had to work just as hard at the same time. Without the great bass tones of the pedals, the rest of the organ sounded thin and anemic. He once gave me a few lessons and, as I struggled to make by fingers perform, I would invariably forget to move my feet at the right time. His expostulation, "Don't forget the pedals! It's not an organ without the pedals!" still rings in my ears.

We have discussed (see Introduction) the two types of God's love which the deuteronomistic historians describe. There is that love which responds to human faith and goodness, and on one level this is the love bestowed upon faithful young Samuel. But God's treatment of Samuel is an expression of that other kind of love, the love which is lavished upon us in good times and in bad, in times of judgment and in times of redemption. Like the deep pedal tones of the organ, the covenant love of God is the foundation upon which the whole house of faith is built. So that even before God removes the offending house of Eli, he has taken steps to prepare young Samuel to lead the nation (see next section). In other words, the judgment of God never takes place in isolation, but is always limited and shaped by his continuing love. By means of this frequent theme 1 and 2 Samuel takes pains to stress that God's act of redemption from judgment is often underway before the act of judgment itself begins.

This is one instance among many which prevents our falling into the trap of claiming that the OT is a book of judgment while the NT is a book of God's love. Judgment-within-love permeates both Testaments and any other understanding is Marcionite mischief.

Samuel's Call (3:1–4:1a)

In the familiar story of Samuel's call more attention has traditionally been given to the lad's experience of the Lord than to the content of the divine revelation. This is not surprising since the condemnation of Eli's family has already just been described by the anonymous seer (1 Sam 2:27–36). However, a more obvious reason for the focus of our attention upon the young Samuel is the tender nature of the scene: the boy keeping vigil beside, or very near, the sacred Ark; his innocence in mistaking the divine voice for that of his old friend; his simple affirmation of trust, "Speak, for thy servant hears" (v. 10). Many generations of young Sunday School children have absorbed this scene and, quite properly, have identified with the awed Samuel, wondering what they might do under similar circumstances, should the voice of the Lord call to them in the night.

We remember, of course, other individuals dramatically called by God: Moses before the burning bush (Exod 3), Isaiah in the Temple shortly after the death of Judah's King Uzziah (Isa 6), Jeremiah in similar circumstances, perhaps not long after the news has come of the death of Assyria's mighty emperor, Assurbanipal (Jer 1:4–19), Ezekiel beside the banks of a river in a strange land, longing for home (Ezek 1), and Paul on the highway to Damascus (Acts 9). Of all of these, however, only the call of Samuel has the quality of a fresh snowfall: chaste, pure. Jeremiah, who complains that the Lord has come to a person too young (Jer 1:6), possesses something of the same quality of innocence, but nothing of the virginal power of young Samuel's awakening.

One minor adjustment to our customary understanding of this important moment in Samuel's life may be in order. The Hebrew writer probably understood the boy to be not the tender, prepubescent child of much of our Sunday School art, but an adolescent of some maturity, say, fifteen to seventeen years of age. The reason for concluding this is that this chapter forms a bridge between Samuel's boyhood proper and his adult ministry, a ministry which comes into its own in the chapter's closing words (vs. 19–21).

The high moment in this pericope is reached when Eli accepts God's word of judgment (thus anticipating his death and that of Hophni and Phinehas in chapter 4) and Samuel is designated a prophet (v. 20). The transfer of spiritual authority is virtually complete and Samuel's new title, when added to those of priest and judge (see 1 Sam 7:15), expressed both the authority granted him by God and the esteem in which he is held by the people. No one since Moses had been viewed as wielding such authority over Israel.

Samuel's three-fold function caused exegetes of an earlier generation to consider him a type of Christ, prophet–priest–judge anticipating the messianic offices of prophet–priest–king. Yet while the person of Samuel is attractive, indeed, we must not forget that the main concern of our text is not with the individual, Samuel, but with the saving activity of God. The key sentence is v. 21, a statement by which our text returns us to the beginning of this narrative. The Lord, who is there described as being virtually absent from Israel's life (v. 1), is now making his presence increasingly felt. In other words, as Samuel reaches adulthood, the Lord uses him as the means of a strong spiritual awakening in the life of the people of God.

So an outline emerges of the theology of chapters 1–3, which tell the tale of young Samuel and also the tale of "The Judge Who Loves."

(1) God's judgment upon the house of Eli has determined its demise.

(2) Even *before* that judgment is delivered, however, God's grace, in a miraculous, or at least unusual action, raises up Samuel, an individual of uncommon strength and devotion.

(3) The ministry of Samuel serves as the catalyst for a spiritual renewal within Israel and under his leadership there emerges a new sense of national purpose and commitment (see 1 Sam 7:3–11).

It should not be assumed, however, that life was made easy for Samuel because of his increasing authority. To be sure, he was doubtless the object of much popular affection, but his labor was difficult and unrelenting (see 1 Sam 7:15–17). In addition, like other men and women of God before and since, Samuel sometimes bore the burden of having to speak to the people words which they wanted least to hear (1 Sam 7:3; 8:10–18; 15:22–23). There is no record to indicate that, as did Jeremiah (Jer 15:10; 20:14–18), Samuel occasionally wished that God had never called him into service. Yet he could be forgiven if he ever felt such emotion, for it is often the lot of the man or woman of God to "sit alone, because thy hand is upon me"(Jer 15:17).

Returning to the outline above of the theology of 1 Sam 1–3, a sermon may be crafted around point #3 entitled "How Odd of God . . ." (a sermon on points #1 and #2 was suggested in the previous section). One of the classical debates among professional historians and sociologists has to do with the impact upon one another of the individual and society. There have been exponents of the so-called "Great Man Theory of History" which states that the course of human events is determined by unusually powerful and influential individuals who arise from time to time to make of human history what it is: Julius Caesar, Jesus of Nazareth, Queen Elizabeth, Thomas Jefferson, and so on. At the other end of the spectrum are those scholars (among whom one would have to include the behavioral psychologists) who believe that, in varying degrees, individual men and women are the products of their environments; that the time was "ripe" for a Julius Caesar or whomever, and that if Caesar had not accomplished the things he did, someone else would have stepped forward to do so.

The debate is obviously complicated and there are no simple answers. Men and women both affect and are affected by social and historical forces. An important note, however, is struck by 1 Sam 3:19–21. As mentioned above, young Samuel's commitment to the Lord becomes the channel by which the Lord increasingly expresses his presence within the life of Israel (another way of translating v. 21 is "the Lord continued to appear at Shiloh"). In other words, the faithfulness of Samuel gives to the Lord an access to Israel's life where such an access had been (at least partially) frustrated before (see v. 1).

A frequent refrain in 1 & 2 Samuel (and in the Bible generally) is the importance of human faith in the plans God has for his world. How odd that God should permit himself to be circumscribed in this manner! How odd that God would lean so heavily upon frail, mortal flesh! How odd that God would become incarnate in a Bethlehem manger! Whether we are totally comfortable with the idea or not, God needs his people, both collectively and individually, to share his tasks and to make their fulfillment possible.

The Fortunes of the Sacred Ark (4:1b—7:2)

In a series of tales we follow the adventures surrounding the Ark of the Covenant. The sacred object which has been carried into battle by the beleaguered Hebrews (4:3), is captured by the Philistines (4:11), only to inflict severe punishment upon them (5:1–12—perhaps a form of bubonic plague) before being returned to the delighted Hebrews (6:1–12). Yet even in Israel its power continues to be deadly, as the citizens of Beth Shemesh painfully discover (6:19–21). It is small wonder that the Ark is allowed a long period of virtual neglect before being reclaimed by David (7:1–3, see 2 Sam 6:2–15). During the course of these tumultuous events, Eli and his sons die and the old sanctuary at Shiloh seems to have been destroyed (see Jer 7:12; 26:6).

This curious set of stories is another point in 1 Samuel where many modern readers of the Bible feel themselves to be looking into a distant, alien world. Newton and Pasteur, Darwin and Freud, reinforced by armies of their brilliant successors, have decisively and forever changed the landscape of the human consciousness so that it is almost impossible for many of us to enter the spirit of terror generated among Philistines and Hebrews alike by the presence of the Ark. We know that objects, including idols, do not fall over for supernatural reasons, but because of forces having to do with gravity and the mutual attraction of bodies. We also know that rational causes lie behind epidemics of disease and infection. And so we have plucked the sting from such stories as 1 Sam 4:1b–7:2.

Have we also, however, plucked from this passage its wonder and awe? Have we deflowered the sense that human life stands before an unfathomable mystery which, while it may never be understood, must at least be "met" if men and women are to live in peace with themselves and with one another?

A basic theological concern lies behind these strange tales of the Ark and its deadly effect upon those around it, a concern relating to the holiness of God. (See Introduction for a discussion of the concept of the "holy" in 1 and 2 Samuel.)

Our world seems to have little sense of the "holy," in terms of all that the OT means by that word. Those disciplines which have done so much to free us from the terrors of the past have also contributed to the desacralization of human life in that they have sometimes inspired us to reduce life to forces which can be weighed, measured, and controlled. In its most grotesque expression this plunder of the sacred led the Nazis to attempt the extermination of an entire race through mass murder and the creation of another by means of Hitler's Aryan baby farms. Yet in less horrible ways the attempted reduction of the sacred goes on all around.

There is something in human nature, however, which resists this effort to expunge the "holy." When men and women are robbed of a sense of mystery about life, they will often create one, except that the substitute is frequently a poor counterfeit of the original. The rise of cults, many of which exhibit a preoccupation with magic and the occult, and the proliferation in our society of the use of hallucinogens are but tragic efforts by men and women, often the young, to build a world of mystery and transcendence to replace the one that has been taken from them.

And so we have "A Tiger by the Tail" and a sermon around that theme might have the following outline: (1) We have all encountered those persons who have attempted to reduce the human experience to elements which can be quantified. Such an individual may be the "mad scientist" of the horror movie, the thorough-going materialist who is motivated only by the acquisition of wealth, or the modern "technocrat" who attempts to translate human experience into computer language. In one way or another, the Frankenstein movies, political systems based solely upon regulated greed, and Orwell's *1984* all remind us that efforts to translate human life into systems of logic and control may pave the way for countless forms of tyranny.

(2) On the other hand, attitudes toward life (including attitudes toward technology and politics), which understand that life is lived as a part of a mystery which the human mind will never be able to understand, but which must somehow be engaged, possess great potential for good. This is the attitude which is willing to leave "open spaces" in life through which the mystery may express itself. Poetry, music, and faith in God may occur only in those "open spaces." The same is true of that political liberty which allows the freedom of speech and the right to dissent. In an age of genetic engineering and of nuclear power these "open spaces" are all the more crucial. They may, indeed, become the means by which life itself is preserved.

(3) Those Hebrews of long ago who laughed at the news of the Philistine's terror before the power of the sacred Ark may seem insufferably naive alongside the modern conception of the manner in which the world functions. Yet perhaps we who live in our desacralized, quick-fix society should pause before we write them off as superstitious bumpkins. Unless there is some focus in our experience upon the "holy," there is much evidence to suggest that our individual lives and the life of society as a whole will be diminished. This element of the holy may take the form of a concern for the hungry or the oppressed. It may be expressed as a commitment to the propagation of beauty in all its forms (one caveat, however: remember that one of the most vigorous collectors of art in our century was the Nazi Hermann Goering). While those who find the ultimate expression of God's love in Jesus Christ will discover in their response to him that framework for the penetration of the holy into their lives.

(A brief note: In preaching on the theme of holiness, one should remember that, in many quarters, the word has a negative connotation, as in "holier than thou." This is because the biblical view of holiness as moral integrity has been both cheapened and misunderstood in our time. Any effort to deal with the concept of the holy in a homiletic manner should take that misunderstanding into consideration.)

Samuel Rallies the People (7:3-17)

Israel has now been stripped of all her powers—except one. With her militia still smarting from the humiliation at Ebenezer (chap. 4), with her towns and countryside under the control of the Philistines, and with her most sacred sanctuary at Shiloh no longer in possession of the Ark, only her faith in God is now a force for good in her life. And at this critical moment Samuel evokes that faith in order to save his people.

Samuel, doubtless despirited because of the death of his old friend and mentor, Eli, now appears at the ancestral home of his parents in Ramah. It is from that place, or more precisely, from the nearby religious center of Mizpah, that Samuel now steps forth to rally his people. The priest is convinced, now that Israel's military might has failed her, that she must seek the real source of her strength, her relationship with God. And so, first demanding that the people remove the idolatrous practices they had learned from their Canaanite neighbors, Samuel calls for a grand assembly of the nation at Mizpah. There he presides over the ritual acts which symbolize the nation's confession of its sin and recommitment to its God.

The Philistines, however, who warily watch for every sign of restlessness among their subjects, take a negative view of these proceedings which, for all they know, may be a preamble to armed insurrection. They therefore gather their forces for a strike against Mizpah and, for the moment, it looks as if the Israelites are to be subjected to new suffering and degradation.

This time, however, the enemy is repulsed, and the editors who were responsible for the final shape of 1 Sam 7 want to be sure that we, the readers, do not miss the point. That which turns the tide of battle is not military arms, but *prayer* and the *faith* that lies behind that prayer. And to make sure that we do not let the message elude us, they report that at the conclusion of the rout of the Philistines Samuel dedicates a monument to the events of this day. It is a stone which he names Ebenezer, that is, "Help-stone" or "Stone of Help." The other Ebenezer (chap. 4), where Israel had relied upon feats of arms, had proved a false "Help-stone." Only here, where the Lord had delivered his faithful trusting people, could be found the true stone worthy of the name.

Samuel then presides over the affairs of the rejuvenated nation. Three times in vs. 15–17 the Hebrew text uses the verb *shaphat*, usually rendered in English by "to judge." This is the term used to describe the activity of those leaders of Israel who guided the affairs of the nation after the Conquest and whose exploits are described in the biblical book which bears their name, Judges. In identifying Samuel as one of these judges, our passage wishes to stress that, as Israel's most important priest at this time, Samuel also stood in the tradition of the great judges of old who, by means of God's special grace, had saved the nation in her darkest hours. As it is to turn out, Samuel will be the last of the judges, the bridge between that fading era in Israel's history and the period of the monarchy about to begin.

1 Sam 7 deals with a theme which is found in many parts of the OT: the crucial role of faith in the life of the people of God. This chapter is similar to Hezekiah's prayer in Isa 37 (see 2 Kings 19) after which the angel of death decimates the invading Assyrian army. In Jer 7 that prophet delivers an astonishing sermon in a time of great international tension in which he declares that Israel's security lies not in smug self-assurance, but in faith in God and in a commitment to justice and mercy. And in 2 Chron 20 an invading enemy force is turned back from the gates of Jerusalem not by an Israelite army, but by the massed choirs of temple singers who confront the aggressors with psalms and hymns.

The OT writers, it must be remembered, seldom, if ever, wrote history just for the sake of telling a story. They wrote it primarily to demonstrate the compassionate, righteous activity of God in the life of Israel and, beyond that, in the life of all humankind. And so, a narrative such as 1 Sam 7 should be understood by us less as a newspaper account (that is, what happened?) and more as spiritual reflection (what does this event tell us about God?). And in this story of the "Second Ebenezer" God's activity is tightly linked to the people's faith and trust, or more specifically to the faith and trust of Samuel, the representative before God of the people.

"Ebenezer Revisited." Prayer and the singing of hymns may seem strange weapons in an age of intercontinental ballistic missiles and hydrogen bombs, an age which would quickly determine that the Mormon Tabernacle Choir would be no match for a division of Red Army tanks. And the radical nature of the biblical proclamation seems all the more so when we remember that, in its own way, the world of the OT Hebrews was no less dangerous a place to live than our own. There is enough bloodshed in the Books of Samuel alone to remind us of the vulnerable position of life and happiness in old Israel and of the violent context in which the human enterprise was carried out in the ancient world.

For this reason the sharp contrast between the hostile approach of the Philistines and the prayerful response of Samuel must be understood as intentional. The message is clear: the ultimate defense in human life, that final force which maintains the integrity of individuals and of nations is faith in God. Closely allied to that faith is a repudiation of violence and of all devices by which human beings seek to maim and to destroy, to degrade and to humiliate other humans.

We should not be led to believe that the final editors of 1 Sam 7:3–17 embraced the naive hope that words of prayer exercised some magic power over swords and chariots. This story, as well as the similar ones referred to above, is rather a paradigm of faith. The sword may indeed kill, but the power of faith would live on and ultimately triumph, even if those who exercised the faith would not always see the fulfillment of that triumph. In our own time examples of this commitment would, of course, include Gandhi and King, as well as unnumbered individuals of lesser fame who seek to live lives of godly peace in the midst of the world's violence. Like Gandhi and King they often pay for their faith with their lives.

In biblical terms, the climax of this theme is the NT announcement of the death and resurrection of Jesus Christ. He is God's promise that faith will survive the sword, not because of the superior strength of the believer, who is frequently crushed, but because of the presence of God.

Thus the two Ebenezers stand in contrast to one another in the mind of the editors of 1 Sam 7:3–17. Only as one joins

Samuel at the Second Ebenezer can the words of Jesus make any sense at all: "Ask, and it will be given you; seek, and you will find; knock, and it will be opened to you" (Matt 7:7) or "If you have faith as a grain of mustard seed, you will say to this mountain, 'Move from here to yonder place,' and it will move; and nothing will be impossible to you" (Matt 17:20).

The Rise of Saul
(1 Samuel 8:1—15:35)

A series of eight chapters chronicles the rise (and partial fall) of Saul. Israel's demand for a king (chap. 8) initiates the action, which continues as Samuel reluctantly anoints Saul to high office (9:1—10:16), the people ratify the divine choice (10:20–24), and God "clothes" Saul with special charismatic gifts (11:1–15). Yet no sooner does Saul's position seem secure than it begins to crumble (chaps. 12 following).

Israel Demands a King (8:1–22)

This passage is one of the crucial texts in the Books of Samuel, because it dramatizes the gathering political crisis with which Israel is now forced to deal. The old way of doing things is proving to be inadequate for the new and changed circumstances in which the nation finds itself. Until this moment Israel has been ruled by her judges, men and women who, gifted by God for special tasks, stepped forth to respond to the crises in the nation's life. The line, however, now seems to be coming to a dead end for, just as Hophni and Phinehas proved to be unworthy successors to their father Eli, so Samuel's own two sons, Joel and Abijah, are not made of the stuff to be heroes for God. And all the while the Philistine menace, in spite of Samuel's good offices, threatens to devour Israel and to demolish her integrity as a nation forever.

And so, in a move which should have surprised no one, leaders from Hebrew communities scattered across the land come to Samuel's home at Ramah to ask for a king. They want to be ruled "like other nations" by a monarch who will "fight our battles" (v. 20). In other words, now that Samuel is approaching the end of his life (or so it seems), the nation desperately needs some individual capable of galvanizing its energies so that the more tightly organized, better equipped Philistines can be held at bay.

On military grounds the suggestion contains a certain

logic, but Samuel senses deep trouble ahead. There is no reason to believe that a Hebrew king will not oppress his people
as the rulers of other nations oppress theirs, and Samuel
foresees a time when freedom loving Israel will be enslaved
by her own ruler. Beyond that, Samuel suspects spiritual difficulties also. Israel's closeness to her God has been thus far
preserved, in part, by her theocratic form of government
which maintained that the Lord was her only king and that
human instruments through whom he worked, such as Samuel, were just that and nothing more. For Israel now to be
ruled by a human king would be as if a cloud were to pass
between Israel and her God, for the human monarch would
surely usurp many of the prerogatives of—and Israel's loyalties to—her divine King.

It is a torturing dilemma, but the urgencies of human life
are strong. And so Samuel is instructed by God to honor the
request, but not before painting a grim picture of things to
come (vs. 10–18).

Israel never really solved the dilemma portrayed here.
Although the institution of the monarchy, especially under
David, saved the nation from its enemies and, under Solomon, gave undreamed prosperity, Israel was always haunted
by the realization that this institution, which was essentially
secular in its ways, killed something of her old intimacy with
her God. And that anti-royalist sentiment which had been
voiced so long before by Gideon (Judg 8:22–23) and repeated
here by Samuel, was to find new expression in the taunt of
the prophet Hosea three centuries later (Hosea 13:10–11).
Here at Ramah, however, the die is cast. With the reluctant
cooperation of the Lord and his servant Samuel, Israel opts
for a king.

"Fireworks for the Fourth of July." The question of government has always been a difficult one for the people of
God. The two bodies of opinion in 1 Samuel, one against the
monarchy, the other in its favor (see Introduction), reflect
genuine tension in early Israel over this matter, a tension
which endured until the collapse of the monarchy in the
Southern Kingdom early in the sixth century B.C. In more recent times the tension has taken different forms. Frequently,
those who have identified themselves as God's people have,

in the effort to give God's rule greater immediacy, succeeded only in imposing new tyrannies: the Puritans of New England, the Ayatollahs of Iran. (Are there those on the "Christian Right" who now present the same danger? Is the dictatorship of communism basically a theocratic tyranny from which God has been removed?) Thus the questions raised by 1 Sam 8 have a current relevance. Government has a responsibility to meet the needs of its people, not to exploit them. That people which invites exploitation will be unhappy. That government which practices it is sowing the seeds of its own destruction.

Samuel Anoints Saul Prince (9:1—10:16)

1 Samuel 9–11 describe the steps by which Israel's demand for a king is realized. It seems apparent to most scholars that the material contained in this part of our narrative is the result of a sewing together of a variety of earlier sources and a good bit of attention has been devoted to the task of identifying the seams. For our purpose, however, it is sufficient to notice that in the arrangement of the final editors the process by which Saul becomes Israel's first monarch is marked by three distinct stages: Saul is anointed prince by Samuel (9:1—10:16), Samuel's private confirmation of Saul is ratified by the people who acclaim the latter man king (10:20–24), and finally the Lord seals the issue by endowing Saul with that *charisma* by which he wins his first important battle (11:1–15). Thus, one might look upon chapters 9–11 as a three act play within the larger drama which constitutes all of 1 & 2 Samuel.

The first act (9:1—10:16) is a narrative of considerable fascination in its own right. The story itself is straightforward enough. Saul, a son of a Benjaminite family of some substance, goes on a quest to recover his father's strayed livestock. In the process, he comes to Samuel who has been alerted by the Lord to expect the arrival of his anointed-to-be. When Saul shows up to enlist the aid of Samuel's clairvoyant powers in locating the animals, Samuel anoints him prince over Israel and confirms the deed by means of a series of unusual events.

Within this uncomplicated structure, however, are em-

bedded details of interest, the complexity of some of which
are only hinted at by our story. First, there is the matter of
Saul's physical appearance. V. 2 informs us that he was
handsome and very tall, and the wording of the final phrase
seems to imply something regal in his bearing. Saul looked
the king! (see 10:23).

Another personal note has to do with the mission which
called Saul out into the countryside, that of hunting his father's lost asses. Even for those in old Israel who had accu-
mulated some wealth life was filled with hard work and was
lived close to the land. David's similar origins come to mind
here, of course, as do the very different conditions which prevailed only a short time later during the opulent period of
Solomon's reign.

More complicated is the sketchy portrait this passage
yields of the nature of the prophetic office at this point in
Israel's life. In some ways the comments concerning the role
of the prophet raise more questions than they answer. V. 9
implies that divine clairvoyance, considered "now" (the time
of the writer) to be a prophetic gift, was formerly the function of the seer. On the other hand, prophecy proper was then
a matter of ecstatic trances, dances, and speech (see 10:9–13).
The manner in which these and other qualities were ultimately fused into the prophetic office as understood by
Amos, Jeremiah, and others, is a question of great interest
and debate. However, in this regard the point of 10:11 is unmistakable. God had laid his hand on Saul in such a way that
he had become transformed.

Of similar interest is the description in our passage of
the relationship between ritual sacrifice, as practiced by Samuel, and the community meal associated with that sacrifice
(9:11–14). The peace offering as described in Lev 7 seems to
be involved here (see 1 Sam 1:4), but Saul's participation in
the meal (9:22–24) entails more than the simple fact that he
was, as a member of the community, entitled to this food.
The suggestion of the text may be that his eating of this special food formed a prelude to his anointing as a prince, perhaps in a manner analogous to the way in which coronation
ceremonies in medieval Europe were often structured
around the Christian eucharist. The fact that the Hebrew text

of 9:22–24 is ambiguous at points does not help in our interpretation of these verses.

Finally, it should be noted that this passage does not use
the usual word for king (*melek*) when speaking of Saul. It pre-
fers a word (9:16, 10:1) which is often rendered "prince" (so
RSV), but which more literally means "the one who is con-
spicuous" or "up front" (*nagid*). Whatever this choice of vocabulary may have implied when this narrative circulated
independently, it has been used by the final editors of 1 & 2
Samuel as a means of stating that Saul's new status as *nagid*
renders him a kind of "apprentice king," subject to the ratifi-
cation by the people (10:24) and the bestowal of the divine
charisma (11:1–15).

The theological message of 1 Sam 9:1—10:13 is pristine
in its clarity: God has heard the cry of his people (8:5,
19–20) and has responded in love. Therefore, we may affirm
that "That Unblinking Eye on the Dollar Bill" is an eye of
love.

When I was a boy a large metal sign on which was paint-
ed a single, staring human eye hung outside the shop of our
town's optometrist and could be seen for blocks. Whenever I
was within sight of that sign I always felt that I was being
spied upon by some malevolent presence. The traditions of
both OT and NT affirm that I was half right: the Presence is
at hand, but he is one of unbounded grace. For this reason
the Church early on embraced the portrait of a human eye as
a symbol for the presence of God (refer to the back of a dollar
bill where the symbol has been incorporated into the Seal of
the United States). Behind this lay such an experience as that
of Abraham who, following the deliverance of Isaac, named
the spot "The Lord Will Provide" (Gen 22:14—literally: "The
Lord Will See").

The theme of 1 Sam 9:1—10:16 is that God provides for
(lovingly sees) the needs of those who trust him. Sometimes
the nature of that provision is surprising. Instead of relief
from his "thorn in the flesh" (2 Cor 12:7) Paul received
strength to endure it so that he became responsive to the
sufferings of others. Sometimes the form of God's providential grace is spoiled by our own sinfulness and human limi-
tations, Saul himself being an example. Yet the experience
of God's people is that his grace is expansive and persistent.

Saul Becomes King (10:17—11:15)

Acts two and three of the mini-drama which describes Saul's progression to the office of king (see above) unfolds as he is confirmed in his office by the people (10:17–27) and then is endowed with that *charisma* which is both the sign of the Lord's blessing and ties him to Israelite leaders of old (11:1–15; see the story of Gideon, esp. Judg 6:11–18).

The passage 10:17–27 is, most scholars are agreed, composed of material from at least two major sources. Vs. 17–19 represents the same anti-royalist stratum present in chap. 8 and, the yet to be discussed, chap. 12. Here once more Samuel denounces the people for the choice they have made in demanding a king and equates their act with spiritual rebellion. The balance of the passage is less hostile toward the idea of monarchy, but it does report the negative comments of some of Saul's acquaintances in his home town of Gibeah (10:27). In a manner which anticipates Jesus' reception by his fellow citizens of Nazareth (Mark 6:1–5), Saul is ridiculed by certain of his neighbors when he returns home following his popular acclaim by the nation. This seems to be less a "put down" of the idea of monarchy than it does the expression of the sentiment "How can this ordinary fellow we've known all our lives lead the nation out of its distress?" (see Luke 4:22). This hostility sets the stage for what subsequently becomes Saul's first act of leniency as king.

The key verse in this passage is 24. After Saul has been singled out by a series of lot takings, the precise nature of which we are ignorant, and after the chosen young man has attempted to hide among the baggage of these pilgrims who have traveled to assemble at Mizpah, only to be ferreted out by the Lord himself (again, the details of the Lord's involvement in v. 22 leave us in puzzlement), Saul is proclaimed king (Hebrew: *melek*) by the assembled representatives of the nation. Thus the "apprentice king" (see above) is now king indeed, and only lacks some opportunity to exercise his royal status.

When the young monarch does act (11:1–15), it is to assume the role of the warrior-king which the people had initially held up as the model of what their ruler should be (8:20). Yet curiously, Saul's first opponent in battle is not the

Philistines, whose threat to Israel had precipitated the present political crisis, but the Ammonites, a Semitic tribe who lived east of the Jordan River (and whose memory is enshrined in the name of the present capital of the Kingdom of Jordan: Amman). The village of Jabesh in the Gilead hills was inhabited by Hebrews who in the past had demonstrated a certain aloofness from the main body of the tribes (Jud. 21:8–12). Perhaps the Ammonite king Nahash was counting on this tradition to make his task easier, or he may have been emboldened by what he perceived to be the precarious position of the infant Hebrew monarchy. However that may have been, the arrogance of the conditions he lays upon Jabesh (v. 2) and his posture of allowing the citizens an unusual amount of time to arrange their defenses indicate that Nahash felt himself the master of the situation.

Saul's reaction to the news from Jabesh was forever to cement his memory in the consciousness of the people of that community, even after his ungracious fall from power. His violent dismembering of the hapless oxen (v. 7) has been viewed by some as having ritual overtones, since the verb translated "cut in pieces" is occasionally applied to the priest's carving of a sacrificial animal (e.g., Lev 1:6, 12). More properly, however, this fierce outburst should be tied to the words in the preceeding verse, "And the spirit of the Lord came mightily upon Saul. . . ." The various pictures of Saul which emerge from 1 Samuel all agree that he was a man of flashing temper, moody, quixotic, and mercurial. It is the same temperament which later causes him to hurl his spear at young David (18:11), to murder the priests of Nob (22:11–19), and, in frenzied desperation, to seek the counsel of a witch before engaging the Philistines in a battle that was sure to mean his death (28:8–25). Saul seems to have been one of those forceful characters in human history who remind us that there is a fine dividing line between greatness and madness. That intense energy which now galvanizes him into leadership over the nation will ultimately destroy him, while the urgings of the "Spirit of God" (v. 6) will all too quickly become those of an "evil spirit from the Lord" (16:14, 18:10). Then Saul, loved and hated by Israel, will be gone, and his descendants doomed to follow him into a murky half-oblivion.

The darkness, however, is tomorrow. Today is all sunshine and, caught up in the exuberance of their victory, the people celebrate. Saul's forgiving attitude toward his detractors at Gibeah (v. 13) heightens the festive mood and, in a duplicate of the action of the Mizpah assembly (10:24), the victorious Hebrew army follows Saul back to Benjamin and, at the old sanctuary of Gilgal, reaffirms his rule as the king whom God has sent to deliver his people (11:15). This final element in the story was originally, according to some scholars, a local Gilgal tradition which perhaps did not know of the similar story set at Mizpah. However, it appears that the final editors who shaped 1 Sam 9–11 into the three act drama of Saul's rise to kingship intend 11:15 as a forceful and climactic expression of joy to accompany the fall of the curtain. There is not the slightest hint here of the troubles which lie ahead. There is merely the simple affirmation of great gladness that God has heard the cries of his people and has responded with supreme care and love.

For purposes of preaching a number of themes emerge from this passage which are of relevance for life in any age, and the resourceful preacher will have little difficulty identifying them. Here are three possibilities:

"When We Tarnish the Golden Rule." The comment by the "worthless fellows" in 10:27 is not reported by the editors of 1 and 2 Samuel as a simple bit of isolated information, but as a prelude to the brief notice in 11:12–13. After Saul's victory at Jabesh his admiring followers remember the slur of 10:27 and bring the fellows to Saul for justice. But Saul, who "held his peace" in 10:27, continues his benign reaction in 11:13 by refusing the opportunity to put the men to death. And yet how humiliated and foolish they must have felt! How much they must have wished they could have retracted the remark of 10:27, even if in their hearts they were still jealous or spiteful toward Saul. The snubs and barbs which we attempt to inflict upon others often come home to haunt us. When those whom we attempt to denigrate prove to be more resourceful and capable than we had imagined, then we must eat crow! The Air Corps cashiered General "Billy" Mitchell, yet his foresight proved the value of the aircraft carrier in modern warfare. Jesus, of course, is the ultimate victim of human spite and blindness: "The very stone which the builders rejected has become the head of the corner" (Matt. 21:42). Those who tarnish the Golden Rule frequently become the butt of their own folly.

Another sermon topic might be "God Loves Us ... In Spite of Ourselves!" We have earlier discussed the dual nature of God's love in the understanding of the deuteronomistic historians, that is, that God responds positively to acts of human faithfulness (and negatively to human unfaithfulness), while at the same time passionately loving his people whether they love him or not (see Introduction). It is clear to any careful reader of 1 and 2 Samuel that at least one of the early sources considered the request for a king (8:4) to be a sinful deed, but the final editors of our books allowed that sentiment to stand alongside a different view which considered the monarchy to be the fulfillment of God's will for Israel (esp. 2 Sam 7:1–17). The anti-royalist attitude is expressed forcefully here in 10:17–19. Yet, according to this view, although God repudiates the people's sin, he does not repudiate his people. Rather he meets them in the midst of their need and responds, not in an absolute fashion, but in a manner which is both loving and a concession to their own moral weakness. The astounding implication of this action is that God permits his own conduct to be influenced by the frailty of his people. In other words, God loves us not because we deserve that love (read Deut 7:6–11), but because that's just the way God is, and the shape of his love is contingent upon our own needs and weaknesses. (But note: any sermon on the love of God runs the danger of seducing one's congregation into presuming on that love. The remark of Heinrich Heine should always be kept in mind: "Of course God will forgive me. That's his business!" Needless to say, that is *not* a frame of mind the preacher wishes to encourage.)

A third possibility for a sermon from this section might be entitled simply "Sing Unto the Lord!" The jubilant nature of those verses which close 1 Sam 11 are, as noted above, in stark contrast to the troubles which lie ahead. And it is probably by design that that is the case, for the editors of this material may have wished to make an important statement here about the nature of the human response to the loving presence of God. "Saul and all the men of Israel rejoiced greatly" (v. 15) is doubtless a way of saying that, whatever the sins of the past, whatever the troubles of the future, there is always reason in life for God's people to celebrate. Faith not only produces hope (see comments on 1 Sam 1), but it also creates joy and the acts of worship and thanksgiving performed by Saul and his followers illustrate that fact. Furthermore, it would appear that joy has a power of its own to strengthen the human spirit and, when it is broken and torn, to heal and restore. The preacher may wish to read Norman Cousin's *Anatomy of an Illness* which describes in a moving way the restorative power of celebration and laughter. 1 Sam 11:15 may, of course, be tied to certain Psalms of Thanksgiving (for example, 30, 32, 116, and Jonah 2:2–9) and to various Psalms of Praise (47, 96, 115, 145, 148). Whenever God's people have been true to their calling, they have sung!

Samuel's Farewell Address (12:1–25)

Samuel, who is now "old and gray" (v. 2) and with a long life of service to God and the people of God behind him, delivers a monologue which has all of the characteristics of a farewell address. In some respects, it is similar to the more expansive farewell remarks of Moses (most of Deut 31–33). Like Moses, Samuel recites a litany of God's gracious deeds toward Israel in the past (vs. 6–10; see Deut 31:4–6), he admits his own growing feebleness (v. 2; see Deut 31:2), and he admonishes Israel to be faithful to God in the years ahead (vs. 14–15, 20–24; see Deut 31:7–8). In addition, although Samuel's address is different in content from the remarks of David upon his deathbed (1 Kings 2:1–9), there is a certain similarity of tone between these two speeches also. David also attests his growing feebleness (1 Kings 2:2) and calls for faithfulness in the future (v. 4). However, one remarkable thing about these three farewells is that, whereas Moses and David say their piece and die, Samuel has yet many years to live and a large role to play in shaping the destiny of Israel's young monarchy. It is not until 1 Sam 25:1 that we are given notice of his death, but before that he will have toppled one king and set up another.

To some, therefore, the present passage seems out of place, a dislocation to be credited to the deuteronomistic editors. Such a conclusion, however, misses the theological and psychological force of this chapter. The point is that Samuel *does* intend to retire and to yield his place in the nation's life (although reluctantly) to the new king. He is ultimately prevented from doing so because Saul flagrantly violates (in Samuel's eyes, at least) those commandments which mean spiritual life for Israel and he propels the nation toward those dire consequences foretold in vs. 15, 25. The delay in Samuel's retirement is thus portrayed as an involuntary act, forced upon him by the continuing spiritual crisis of the nation.

Samuel's address contains three major divisions: In vs. 1–5 the old prophet–priest–judge affirms his own moral integrity. Vs. 6–12 are Samuel's recital of God's mighty acts of the past. And vs. 13–25, the most interesting section, spell out Samuel's theological ideal for Israel (see esp. vs. 14–15), and remind the people that in asking for a king they have departed from the traditions of old and have seriously sinned against God (vs. 11–12). In addition, this third section goes on to stress that this sin will return to haunt the nation unless the people remain close to God (vs. 20–25). (This final section is punctuated by a miracle performed by Samuel in which he summons a thunderstorm during the wheat harvest, that is, the month of June, normally a dry period in Israel [vs. 16–19]. Its purpose is to lend divine authenticity to what Samuel is saying.)

A number of scholars have tended to look upon this address as a composition of the deuteronomistic editors. The formula of vs. 14–15 certainly resonates with deuteronomistic language (see Deut 17:14–20), and even the recital of God's role as Israel's defender in the past in vs. 6–11, while not an exclusively deuteronomistic view, does indeed sound like the Book of Deuteronomy (chaps. 1–3; 6:20–25; 26:5–9). Moreover, Israel's later experience of faithless and despotic rulers would have caused the sentiments of much of Samuel's address to be right at home in the period when the deuteronomistic editors worked.

However, while the influence of those editors is not to be dismissed entirely it should not be forgotten that the sentiments expressed by Samuel are precisely those that we would expect the old man to have. Israel has now embarked upon an adventure of which he disapproves. It is, for him, not just a matter of his having been personally displaced, although the wounds to his own pride may have played a part in shaping his feelings. That which was old and dear, that which has proved to be the nation's strength in the past (her loose tribal confederation centered in the worship of God) was to be abandoned for a course which was new, untried, and dangerous. It was hot, young blood lusting for a change which caused gray heads everywhere to shake. Yet to Samuel's credit it must be stressed that he insisted that the nation would continue to do well, even under the evil institution of monarchy, if the people would maintain their closeness to God. V. 20 is the theological lynchpin of the entire chapter, a passage which, in spite of whatever deuteronomistic glosses it may contain, seems quintessentially old Samuel.

"Trust We in God?" 1 Sam 12 wants to know. Change is endemic to human life, and it often pits generations against one another, youth against age. And the question which faces every human society is how much change is required or enough? And in which directions? Not enough growth/change stultifies and dwarfs the organism. Too much is a cancer which kills. And, of course, not all change *is* growth. And so no pat answers emerge, no easy solutions. Each human community, each human individual must struggle to strike the right balance. Yet 1 Sam 12 insists upon qualities which shape the way we change and nurture the way in which we grow. Trust in God is one such quality and, by implication, so is a concern for one's fellow human being (see Matt 22:36–40). "In God We Trust" on our coins should perhaps be broadened to continue "And for Each Other We Are Concerned."

Another sermon, this one for Lent, might bear the title "The Love Which Gives" and focus on v. 23. Samuel's comment is that he will not cease to pray and work for his people in spite of the fact that he understands their request for a king as a personal rejection of his own leadership (see 8:7 which implies such an attitude on Samuel's part, an attitude which may also be sensed behind the words of 12:1–5). In other words, although the people have turned their backs upon Samuel and upon his ideals for Israel, he will not retaliate in kind, for to repay rejection with rejection would be to sin against God. And so, in putting his own hurt aside,

Samuel continues to love his people and to intercede for their well-being before God. Anyone who has ever been in Samuel's position will know how difficult it is. (1) Our natural tendency is to repay others in kind. The newspapers frequently carry stories of scorned lovers who maim or kill because their love is rejected. As a high school student I was shocked into an awareness of the power of this love/hate emotion when an acquaintance who sat directly behind me in an English class murdered the father of his fiancée with a shotgun because the man wanted to prevent the marriage of his daughter to my classmate. Even when it implies no physical hostility, our usual response to rejection frequently hurts other people, including ourselves. (2) Yet the prophetic word in the Bible summons us to rise above such destructive and tragic reactions. In 1 Sam alone we have not only this example of Samuel himself, but also the model of David's gentle treatment of a vengeful Saul (24:1–7; 26:6–12) and of Jonathan's continuing love for the man who would replace his father (and, by implication, himself) upon the throne (20:42). This is a different order of love, and Jesus' words upon the cross, "Father, forgive them; for they know not what they do," (Luke 23:34) are perhaps the ultimate expression of that love. To love without hope of return is the highest form of love. (3) Lent is a time, not only of self-searching and repentance, but also of self-giving. It is a season for rededication to all that Christ had to say about turning the other cheek and going the second mile (Matt 5:38–42). It is a season for cultivating the ability to give of oneself even when that giving (or loving) is not reciprocated. There is no logic which may argue that such radical imperatives "ought" to be done. The only logic here is that of a loving God who gave his Son even when he knew his gift would be pinioned to a cross.

Samuel Condemns Saul: First Episode (13:1–15a)

Hardly has Saul begun to rule than he runs afoul of Samuel, whose misgivings about the institution of monarchy have just been reported in some detail in the preceeding chapter. The condemnation which Samuel imposes upon Saul, however, seems in many respects unjust, as we shall presently discuss.

First, a few comments about details in this chapter. The Hebrew text of v. 1 is corrupt in that the numeral relating to Saul's age at this time has been lost. Considering that he was the father of a fighting son, however, he could not have been much younger than forty, and was probably older. As to the duration of his reign, two years (so the Hebrew text) does not seem too short a time, especially if one reckons the end of his effective rule as the time of the anointing of David, the probable view of the deuteronomistic historians. On the other hand, some scholars feel that a longer time is demanded and that a numeral has fallen out of the Hebrew text at this point also (cf. RSV).

Vs. 2–7 briefly tell the tale of the first recorded encounter between an army of Saul (this one commanded by Jonathan) and the Philistines, together with the repercussions of that conflict. Since the native Canaanites had been all but eliminated as a military presence, the Philistines were now the most serious threat to the safety of the Israelite communities scattered through the central Palestinian hill country. These people, who had invaded the southern coastal plain at about the same time the Hebrews under Joshua were entering the land from the east, were descendants of Aegean groups who had been displaced from their own homelands some time earlier. They had entered this land to which they ultimately gave their name ("Palestine" is a different form of "Philistine") after having been repulsed by the forces of the Egyptian pharaoh Ramses III following an abortive effort to settle in Egypt. They thus represented a higher level of technological achievement than the Hebrews (note 1 Sam 13:19–21) and posed a mortal danger to the Israelite tribes.

Following the battle of Aphek-Ebenezer (1 Sam 4), the Philistines appear to have imposed themselves upon the central hill country and, in spite of such comments as those in 1 Sam 7:13–14, they dominated the Hebrew settlements there, plundering Hebrew goods, taxing Hebrew produce and, in general, rendering Hebrew life miserable. The defeat of the Philistine garrison at Geba (north-central Benjamin, the heart of the hill country) by Jonathan's contingent sent shock waves through both Philistine and Hebrew hearts, because it meant that the cruel Philistine rule was being challenged.

As expected, the Philistines retaliate with a large army

(vs. 5–7), and the Hebrews are scattered. The movements of
Saul during this episode are not clear. In v. 2 he is at the
head of a body of 2,000 men at Michmash (on the Benjamin-
Ephraim border), but in v. 5 the Philistines are in control of
Michmash, while Saul is "still in Gilgal" (v. 7), the cultic
center in east Benjamin which was the site of the coronation
celebration following the relief of Jabesh (11:14–15) and an
area intensely loyal to Saul. Saul was thus either driven from
Michmash by the Philistines or, more probably, withdrew to
Gilgal to muster his forces.

   The stage is now set for a military showdown, but a tragic event intervenes. Because Saul wants God's blessing upon
himself and his army, he delays engaging the Philistines until Samuel can arrive to offer sacrifices. When seven days
have elapsed and Samuel has still not arrived, Saul finds
himself in a precarious dilemma: he must either continue to
delay while the strength of his army is destroyed by attrition
(v. 11), or he must seize the priestly office to which he had
not been ordained and offer the sacrifices himself. He has no
sooner chosen the latter alternative than old Samuel appears
to denounce him. And the priest not only rebukes Saul, but
condemns him to political (and spiritual) death by declaring
that the favor of God has been withdrawn from Saul and
transferred to someone else. Saul still has a role to play in
Israel's life, of course, but the reader of 1 Samuel is in no
doubt about the ultimate fate of this monarch. He is doomed
because he broke the commandment of God (v. 13).

   And yet it all seems so unjust. Saul has not acted in a fit
of passion, but has rather demonstrated uncharacteristic pa-
tience in waiting a full week for Samuel to come to the army.
Samuel, in fact, seems more culpable than Saul, and the
modern reader will not escape the suspicion that the old
priest, smarting over his lost authority in Israel's life, has
seized upon a pretext to rid himself of a rival whom he intensely dislikes. Many of David's sins, after all, are to be far
more heinous than those of Saul, and some, as here, even involve "sacramental" matters. (For example, read 1 Sam
21:1–6 and note Jesus' forgiving attitude toward the incident
in Matt 12:3–4.) Yet David is not deprived of his kingdom!
Why could there not be some note of mercy in Samuel's re-

sponse to Saul? Why could not this strong king be forgiven and saved?

Such questions pose a dilemma for the preacher, and one should beware of the temptation to slip into shallow and false moralizing in dealing with this text. (Such as: Saul is an example of an unrepentant heart which God has no choice but to destroy.) The truth is that we stand here before a mystery. It is a historical fact that Saul did not succeed as Israel's first king, and this passage is one of the explanations which the OT gives concerning the reason why. Yet because the theology expressed here seems inadequate when compared to the higher theology of our Lord, we must acknowledge the limited ability of this text to speak an authoritative word about God to the men and women to whom we must preach.

Victory at Michmash (13:15b—14:52)

In an extended narrative the events surrounding the great Israelite victory at Michmash are described, and to this account are added two stories of a personal and theological nature involving King Saul, together with miscellaneous notes relating to the life and conduct of the court. In outline the entire section looks something like this:

Prelude to battle: 13:15b–23
The battle proper: 14:1–23
Two stories concerning Saul's faithfulness: 14:24–46
Jonathan and the forbidden honeycomb:
14:24–30, 36–46
The affair of the unclean meat: 14:31–35
Miscellaneous notes: 14:47–52
Saul's victories: 14:47–48
Saul's family and associates: 14:49–51
Saul's charismatic appeal: 14:52

This outline, together with a reading of the text itself, reveals the section to be composed of material from a variety of sources.

Concerning the battle, the predominant theological motif is that this is a victory whose architect is God alone. In other words, the rout of the Philistines at Michmash is another evidence that God is the protector and defender of his people. Several elements in the story converge to underscore this theme. The notice of the technological disadvantage of the Hebrews in 13:19–22 renders even more graphic the information concerning their numerical disadvantage (600 Hebrew warriors—13:15b, 14:2—against 30,000 chariots, 6,000 horsemen, etc—13:5). When the initial skirmish is joined it is two Hebrews against 20 Philistines (14:14). Yet according to Jonathan, the presence of the Lord causes numbers to be irrelevant (14:6). The manner in which Jonathan refers to the Philistines as "these uncircumcised" (14:6) suggests the language of the holy war. The fashion in which the Philistines react to their first sight of Jonathan and his armor-bearer is interpreted as a sign from God: "The Lord has given them into the hand of Israel" (14:12).

The prominence of Jonathan in the battle and the low profile accorded Saul may be more than a simple "human interest" element. This feature of the story perhaps suggests that the curse of Samuel (13:13–14) is already beginning to take its effect. Having been denounced by the elderly priest, Saul is forced to take a back seat in this important victory to his energetic first-born son. In this way, the condemnation of Israel's first king is limited to him alone, while the well-being of the nation as a whole is not compromised.

If such a statement is being made by the passage 14:1–23, this view of Saul is certainly not shared by the remainder of chap. 14. The two stories in 14:24–46 seem to be included here for the primary purpose of saying a good word about the faithfulness of Saul to the commandments of God. The first of these narratives (vs. 24–30, 36–46) draws upon the understanding in early Israel that vows taken during the progress of a holy war are binding before God. (It is interesting to compare this story with the tragic account of Jephthah's vow under similar circumstances in Jud 11:29–40. In both stories, the willingness of the child to die [Jud 11:36, 1 Sam 14:43] in order to preserve the integrity of the father's vow serves to heighten the pathos.) The point is: Saul is willing to sacrifice Jonathan in order to be found obedient before God. Interrupting the first story is a second (14:31–35) which illustrates Saul's zeal for obeying the regulation of Lev 17:10–14 concerning the eating of blood.

Moreover, of the three brief notices which conclude chap. 14, one (vs. 47–48) describes Saul's success as a warrior-king, and another (v. 52) his success at attracting fighters to his ranks. In sum, the passages in 14:24–52 portray a different Saul from the king whom Samuel has condemned, and perhaps a different monarch from the one suggested in 14:1–24. Here, Saul is every inch the warrior-king, decisively leading his armies into battle and carefully obeying the laws of God.

At least two possible themes emerge from this extended passage 13:15b—14:52. "The Victories of God" is a frequent OT motif which reminds us not only of our dependence upon God, but of our need for humility in the face of personal accomplishments. Jonathan's bravery in facing the Philistines virtually alone is balanced by his awareness that his success is not due only to skill of arms or strategy (an ambush is suggested by 14:4–5). His sense of the presence of God (v. 12) places the great victory in perspective, and implies both spiritual and psychological health on the part of the young man. Why is it that, in a success oriented society like our own, personal achievements (fame, wealth) are often accompanied by spiritual disorientation and mental unhealth? Is it because the battles we fight are often not those of God? Is it because the victories (especially the worthwhile ones) "we" win are not just because we were strong or clever, yet we do not acknowledge our own limited role in "our" accomplishments?

Another sermon which might be developed along this theme is "Will the Real King Saul Please Stand Up?" An honest reading of 1 Samuel will reveal contrasting opinions about the character of Israel's first king. Even those in a position to judge him best were not in agreement concerning his character and his relationship to God. In an age like our own in which bigotry abounds, the OT's fragmented picture of Saul should serve as an example of how difficult it is to assess other people. The "true Christian" may ultimately be unmasked as an evil tyrant (Elmer Gantry, Jim Jones of Jonestown), while those who quietly do the works of Christ without fanfare may be recognized only by those few persons who are nearest to them. Certainly, ours is a time in which a religious label conveys very little concerning the person who wears it.

Samuel Condemns Saul: Second Episode (15:1–35)

The second narrative in which Samuel denounces Saul for his disobedience to God and declares his rule over Israel to be forfeit is relatively straightforward in its theological reasoning. According to the law of Lev 27:28–29, those persons and things which possess the quality of *herem* (RSV: "devoted thing"), or what we have called "negative holiness" (see Introduction), are to be destroyed. There can be no exceptions to this regulation without compromise to the commitment within Israel to the holiness of God. Therefore, Samuel's demand of Saul that the Amalekites and all of their possessions are to be annihilated, an imperative which seems cruel and wasteful in a modern context, would have been perfectly at home in the time of the early Hebrew monarchy. When Saul disobeys by sparing the life of King Agag (out of hope for a ransom? as an act of pity?) and by allowing his followers to appropriate the goods of the slain Amalekites, he is once again confronted by Samuel and informed that the office of king is to be taken from him (vs. 26–27).

Although chap. 15 seems to be ignorant of the contents of 13:1–15a, especially 15:1 which appears to be a way of reaffirming Saul's kingship, the two passages nevertheless have much in common. Gilgal is the scene of both. In each one Saul receives a command from Samuel which relates to a cultic ordinance. And, of course, in each Saul disobeys, only to be told by Samuel that the kingdom has been taken from him and given to some anonymous person whom the reader knows to be young David. These close structural similarities have occasioned the flow of much scholarly ink as students of this material have attempted to determine the literary connection, if any, between these two passages in their original forms, a debate which need not concern us here. For purposes of theological interpretation, the final editors of 1 Samuel have used the narrative of chap. 15 as a means of reinforcing the point made by chap. 13: Saul proved inadequate to the demands of the office God laid upon him and so, in his concern for Israel, God turned to another.

Of some interest is the fact that the characters in the drama assume more human dimensions in chap. 15 than in 13. Samuel shows little emotion in 13, whereas in 15 he is "angry" (v. 11) and "he cried to the Lord all night." Presumably the focus of that anger is Saul and Samuel's cries are those of rage. (Another, although unlikely, interpretation is that Samuel was angry at the Lord's decision of v. 11a and that his cries are prayers that the Lord will change his mind—but note v. 29.)

Saul also displays more emotion in chap. 15 than in 13. Only in 15 does the king acknowledge his wrongdoing and plead for forgiveness (vs. 24–25). When this is denied to him by an icy Samuel, Saul begs the older man not to leave him, tearing Samuel's clothing in the process. The persistence of Saul finally wins a single grudging concession from Samuel. The old prophet-priest joins the distraught king in the public worship of God.

An additional element in chap. 15 which elevates it over 13 is the dramatic touch in v. 14. When Saul, who has kept the Amalekite king and the spared Amalekite possessions out of Samuel's sight, reports to the older man that he has kept the commandment of the Lord (v. 13), Samuel inquires pointedly, "What then is this bleating of the sheep in my ears . . .?" Saul is undone and his feeble defense is no match for the elder man's ire. Nothing like 15:14 relieves the basically unadorned style of 13:1–15a.

Vs. 22–23 are a poetic insertion into a narrative which is otherwise prose. Because of this sudden change in style as well as because of certain conceptual features (e.g., the Hebrew word "teraphim" in v. 23 [RSV: "idolatry"] is obviously used in a negative sense. But see the nonjudgmental use of the same word in 1 Sam 19:13), vs. 22–23 are considered by many to be a later insertion into the text. The sentiments expressed are consistent with other parts of the OT, such as Ps 50:9, 51:16–17, Hosea 6:6, Micah 6:6–8.

As was observed in the discussion of 13:1–15a, we stand before a mystery. We can accept without difficulty that Saul proved to be an ineffective ruler, especially in light of his quixotic nature which violently asserted itself more frequently with the passage of time. Yet it is difficult to fit the explanation of Saul's demise offered by 1 Sam 15 into our understanding of what Jesus taught concerning the dynamics of repentance and forgiveness, especially in the face of 15:25–26. And again we must raise the name of David. Why was David's repentance in 2 Sam 12:13 accepted and that of Saul rejected?

David Eclipses Saul
(1 Samuel 16:1—31:13)

We now enter a section in which Saul, although still nominally Israel's king, is more and more losing his place to the youthful Judean, David. The section begins with the story of David's secret anointing by Samuel in chap. 16 (16:13 is the first mention in the OT of David's name), and concludes with the account of Saul's death and burial in chap. 31. In the course of the narrative the friction between David and Saul increases, as does the estimation of David in the eyes of the people. Therefore, with Saul's death David is ready to step forward to claim the monarchy.

David's Entrance into History (16:1–23)

David is easily the dominant character in 1 & 2 Samuel and it is therefore not surprising that the narrative of his introduction into Israel's life should be a subject of some interest to those who were responsible for this literature. The story as it stands is composed of two sections: vs. 1–13 in which Samuel, acting circumspectly for fear of Saul's wrath, anoints David to be Israel's king, and vs. 14–23 in which David enters the life of the court as Saul's armor-bearer and personal attendant.

Vs. 1–13 bear a certain resemblance to the narrative of Saul's anointing in 10:1–16. In both episodes Samuel acts at the direction of God who gives the priest a miraculous sign by which he recognizes the divine designee. In both the intended recipient of the anointing is ignorant of what is about to happen. And in both stories the new king, who presumably returns to his normal pursuits, is soon called into a fresh kind of service. Among important differences in the two stories, however, is the fact that, whereas Saul soon begins to "play the king," David's surreptitious anointing is followed by a period in which he is prevented by events from assuming his new office.

The sense of the crucial nature of this moment in Israel's history is heightened by the manner in which David's anointing takes place. An air of some tension is created in vs. 1–5 by the circumstances of Samuel's journey to Bethlehem. It is not clear why the elders of the city should have been afraid of Samuel (v. 4), but their anxiety, coupled with Samuel's own fear of Saul (v. 2), places a cutting edge to the story of what is about to follow. To this must be added the manner of David's selection as a means by which the message is conveyed that an electrifying moment is at hand. The sons of Jesse are passed over one by one until the implied question (v. 11) seems to be "Is God truly going to be able to live up to his promise?" Only then is David summoned, the youngest of the brothers, who was considered too unimportant to be brought in from his sheep to meet the great man of God.

The love affair which Israel was to have over the centuries with the figure of David is reflected in the portrait of the young man given here. Already he has been referred to in flattering tones (13:14, 15:28—in neither place is David's name used), but now the admiration of the writers of 1 & 2 Samuel for Israel's great king expresses itself more pointedly. The description of David's physical beauty in v. 12 (our best clue from the OT as to what he looked like—see 17:42) is followed by a statement in v. 13 concerning his new spiritual state. The anointing by Samuel has been confirmed by God whose Spirit (in some unspecified manner) has now "come mightily" upon David (see Saul's ecstasy in 10:9–13).

The second pericope in this passage (vs. 14–23) tells of the manner in which David moves from tending his father's sheep to functioning as a member of Saul's court. (Another story intended to provide this same information will shortly follow in chap. 17.) Most scholars are agreed that the two sections in chap. 16 originally came from different sources, vs. 1–13 from that cycle of stories concerning Samuel (see Introduction), and vs. 14–23 from that sympathetic to Saul. Nevertheless, the final editors have skillfully spliced the two units together by allowing the statement concerning the conferring of the Spirit of the Lord upon David in v. 13 to provide a contrast to that in v. 14 where we are told that the Spirit of the Lord now left Saul and was replaced by an evil spirit.

The theological questions raised by v. 14 cannot be easily answered, but it may be of some help to note that, at a time before the development within Israel of the concept of a personal Satan, both good *and* evil were often attributed to God. (See, for example, Isa 45:7, a statement from the late sixth century B.C. Also compare the manner in which the Lord permits "The Adversary" to inflict himself upon Job [Job 1:6–12]. In addition, refer to our comments above in discussing 11:6.) The most that can be said with certainty is that Saul's growing derangement, perhaps exacerbated by his conflict with Samuel, is given a theological dimension. It is seen as a further sign that God has withdrawn his support of Israel's first king.

Meanwhile, the new king must wait in the wings until God can bring to pass those events which will allow David to assume that office to which God has called him. The story in vs. 14–23 is intended to underscore the difference between the two men: Saul—rejected by God, morose, evil-tempered, and tormented; and David—God's chosen, brave, sweet-tempered, and strong. David's power over Saul's evil spirit (v. 23) is a forecast of the manner in which the intertwined destinies of these two individuals will play themselves out.

"Promises! Promises!" The theology of chap. 16 seems to be that God will work his will in human life in spite of the fact that those in whom he places his trust sometimes prove unable or unwilling to do those tasks to which he summons them. When Saul proved to be an ineffective king (for whatever human reasons may lie behind the theological explanations of chaps. 13 and 15) God raised up David, and the promise of chap. 16 is that God intends always to keep this trust with his people. Those who do God's will may often be called to champion unpopular causes and to be the object of public hostility. So any preaching based on chap. 16 must avoid the temptation to be "triumphalist." Yet it is a strong source of hope to the men and women of God that God has a manner of identifying and calling those who are to be his spokespersons and the doers of his will. Who are those in our own time upon whom God's Spirit has come mightily? Doubtless many would identify persons like Mother Theresa, Martin Luther King, Jr., Billy Graham, and Pope John Paul II. Yet it must never be forgotten that those who fulfill the promises of God in our midst are also to be found quietly at work in every community. Some of them are surely present in your own parish or congregation.

In addition, there are two statements in chap. 16 which, on their own, may provide homiletic material. The first of these is v. 7 which may generate thoughts on the theme "God and His X-Ray Vision." This text has often been understood in a figurative (or sometimes even literal) sense; that is, God has a way of discovering our true motives and our potential for good or evil when those qualities may be concealed from our fellow human beings. Undoubtedly this is true, and Jesus' own comments to people often made them feel that he was able to see straight through them (see John 4:16–19). But that is only a part of the theological import of this verse. A deeper meaning arises out of the context in which v. 7 lies, that is, the rejection of Saul over which Samuel has deeply grieved (v. 1). And perhaps this meaning furnishes us with a clue concerning the mystery of why Saul was rejected. The basic difference between Saul and David was not that one was sinful and the other virtuous. They were both sinful. Rather, the difference lay in an attitude of their hearts toward God and his ways with Israel (see Introduction). Saul apparently made no effort to keep open the channels of grace between God and himself, while David, in spite of his waywardness, was responsive to God's judgment and love. The difference between the men was thus not what they did, but *who* they were within. And it was ultimately that "within," that quality of their hearts, which determined their destinies (compare Jesus statement in Matt 12:35). That which causes men and women to be what they ultimately become is not just external circumstance, but how we deal with our experiences and how we respond to them. Viktor Frankl, who survived the Nazi death camps, afterwards wrote that the Nazis could deprive their victims of every dignity except one: "the last of the human freedoms—to choose one's attitude in any given set of circumstances—to choose one's own way." The Lord looks upon the heart not simply because of his all-knowing ways, but because that is where the real "we" resides, a "we" which sooner or later becomes evident to everyone.

Another sentence which may be used as a sermon text is v. 11 where a Christmas sermon may be generated around the theme "Our Weakness: His Strength." Here Jesse, in response to Samuel's question, tells the prophet that he has one more son: "There remains yet the youngest, but behold he is keeping the sheep." A frequent theme in the Bible is that God chooses not the strong and powerful to do his work, but the weak and the small. Moses complains of being too dull-witted (Ex. 4:10), and Jeremiah of being too young (Jer 1:7). Samuel was only an adolescent when he heard God's call (1 Sam 3). And God's own son was a baby in a rural stable. David fits that mold. (Notice that Jesse's statement implies that the thought had never crossed his mind that David would prove to be the object of Samuel's search.) He is not only the tenderest of Jesse's sons, but he is a shepherd. To be sure, such an experience would quickly harden a boy into a man (see 1 Sam 17:37), and yet it was not an occupation of distinction. There were thousands of shepherds in the Israel of Samuel. And so the question: why David? There is no answer, of course. Just as the OT sometimes struggles with the "why" of Israel's election without coming to a concrete conclusion (Deut 7:6–8), so individual Christians and the Church as a whole must do the same. There *is* no answer apart from the grace of God, but the fact is that we have been summoned by God to care and to serve. And although God demands that we put our resources at his disposal, he does not call us because we are strong, but because we are weak and helpless. Christmas is a time when we are impressed again with wonder over a God who would attempt to do the most important work in the world with instruments which, in human terms, are the most inadequate.

David and Goliath (17:1–58)

This extended pericope has impressed itself upon the consciousness of the Hebrew-Christian community more forcefully than perhaps any other passage in 1 & 2 Samuel. The spiritually illiterate individual who can tell us little else about the Bible will nevertheless know the bare essentials concerning David and Goliath, a story whose very popularity has made it into a kind of model folk tale which, it is assumed, reminds us that the underdog occasionally wins out over enormous odds. This popularization of 1 Sam 17, however, has little to do with the theology of the narrative as it appears in the OT. The story is not one of the strength (or luck) of the underdog, but rather an affirmation of the power of God. And in preaching from this text, we must be careful not to confuse the two.

Most scholars are convinced that an intriguing literary history lies behind this chapter, although no one can be quite sure what that history is. For one thing, a number of Greek manuscripts contain a version of 1 Sam 17 which is considerably shorter than that of the traditional Hebrew text: omissions include vs. 12–31, 41, 55–58. It is interesting to read the remaining verses (those found both in Greek and Hebrew) and notice that they form a coherent and logical story. Therefore, an interesting debate has arisen concerning which form of the story is older (i.e., was the original Hebrew version shortened by the Greek translators, or was an originally straightforward story embellished with certain details before being incorporated into the Hebrew OT?). This debate is made all the more intriguing by the evidence of the Qumran texts (concerning 1 & 2 Samuel generally, not specifically chap. 17) which suggest that the Qumran scribes and the Greek translators may have worked from "editions" of 1 & 2 Samuel which bore certain features in common not found in the "edition" which lies behind the received Hebrew text of these books.

Another feature which suggests that the story of David and Goliath had an independent life before being incorporated into the text of 1 Samuel is the discrepancies between this chapter and the material which surrounds it. Most important of these is the fact that 17:1–58 is written in such a manner as to suggest that the author knew nothing of the events of 16:14–23. (Also see 2 Sam 21:19 which credits the death of Goliath to a certain Elhanan.) Both stories, standing independently, seem designed to answer the question concerning how David first came into the life of the court. Yet lying side by side, they appear contradictory. The conversation between Saul and Abner in vs. 55–56 is illogical in the light of 16:14–23, especially v. 19. Moreover, the notation in v. 54 that David carried Goliath's severed head to Jerusalem appears to be an anachronism, in view of the fact that Jerusalem at this time was still a Jebusite city, yet to be conquered by David and transformed into Israel's capital (2 Sam 5:6–10).

While considerations such as these are important to a critical study of ch. 17, it is essential that we ask the theological purpose of this passage as it now stands in the context of 1 Samuel. Here answers seem more certain. The final editors of 1 Samuel have, as noted above, used this story as a means of making an important statement concerning the power of God. David, who has just been anointed king by Samuel (16:1–13) and who has been brought to court as the personal servant of the deteriorating King Saul, now receives the divine *charisma*. He is endowed with those special gifts of God which, at the same time, present themselves as a symbol of God's presence in the young man's life and, in addition, become the means by which God acts to deliver his people on an important occasion. In the view of the deuteronomistic editors, 1 Sam 17 occupies a similar place in the life of David as Saul's victory over the Ammonites (1 Sam 11:1–15) had occupied in the career of Israel's first king. The "cloak" of God's mighty presence, which had been worn by the judges of old, has now passed from Saul to David.

As stated earlier, it is important that this text not be approached (as it often is) with the idea that it says something like "God is on the side of the underdog." Although the OT affirms in a number of places that the weak and the outcast are a special concern of God (see Hannah's Thanksgiving in 2:1–10), that point is not the one being made here. Rather the message is that God keeps faith with his people. Saul may have proved to be a "broken reed," but God, out of his love for Israel, is raising up a greater than Saul. Perhaps the key verse is 37. As Jonathan had done in 14:12, David acknowledges that the impending victory is to be not his, but God's. And thus in the eyes of the deuteronomists this is not a conflict between David and Goliath, essentially, at least. It is rather a conflict between Goliath and God.

And so we might reflect upon "Poor Little Goliath." Sermons on familiar passages such as this one are, in some respects, the most difficult of all to write and to preach, for the simple reason that one must slice through a tough crust of familiarity before reaching the bread itself. We may be jarred out of our complacency here when we realize that, if this narrative has an underdog, it is not David, but Goliath. His was the misfortune to be pitted not against a green shepherd boy, but against the living God! The outcome was inevitable. What evil and oppressive situations from the past can you think of which were overturned by ordinary people because they turned out to be the champions of a godly cause? What sinful or destructive circumstances are being challenged in your own community by persons who are committed to the will of God? What does 1 Sam 17 say about the dynamics of history in such confrontations? Whom would our story label the "real" underdogs? (Note the caveat concerning those who "do the will of God" in the discussion above of 8:1–22.)

David Waxes While Saul Wanes (18:1—19:24)

These two chapters are composed of a variety of miscellaneous stories which the deuteronomistic editors of Samuel-Kings have brought together and which all have as a common theme Saul's increasing jealousy over the rise to fame of his young compatriot. Because of their obvious fascination to subsequent generations, a large number of anecdotes concerning the Saul-David rivalry must have been preserved, and a selection of them is introduced here in order to illustrate a principal theme of 1 Samuel: God's grace raised up David in response to the disobedience (or, as it may seem to some modern readers, the simple inadequacy) of Saul (see 18:14). We will briefly discuss each of the stories contained in this extended section.

18:1–5: David is retained in service by Saul and a deep, warm relationship is established between David and Jonathan. This passage may be a continuation of 17:55–58, both of which are omitted from important Greek manuscripts. Its main point is contained in v. 5: David became increasingly popular among the Hebrews generally and, in particular, among Saul's own circle. (For a discussion of the important David-Jonathan relationship, see the comments on chap. 20.)

18:6–11: Hebrew women greet David with a song which contrasts him favorably with Saul, much to the latter's anger. Saul then tries to kill David with his spear. The song in v. 7 must have been extremely popular in old Israel, for it is reproduced three times in 1 Samuel (see 21:11, 19:5). Vs. 10–11 are considered by many to be an interpolation on the grounds that they anticipate 19:10 and also that these two verses (unlike 6–9) are missing from many Greek manuscripts.

18:12–16: Saul makes David a military commander with the apparent intention of placing him in great danger. David, however, is very successful and his popular esteem continues to grow. As noted above, v. 14 is specific in crediting David's accomplishments to the Lord.

18:17–19: Saul promises David his daughter, Merab, but later reneges on the agreement. This is probably a brief summary of a longer tale which, in its original form, may have been similar to the narrative of 18:20–30. The fact that Adriel the Meholathite is mentioned as the husband of Michal in 2 Sam 21:8 leaves us in some confusion concerning the actual events behind this passage (see 2 Sam 3:15).

18:20–30: Saul, hearing that his daughter Michal loves David, sets a trap. He promises her to him in return for one hundred Philistine foreskins. When David secures them, Saul is more fearful and enraged than ever. This anecdote, which reads like one of the "labors of Hercules," is another means of driving home the refrain of this section. That is, the Lord is responsible for David's successes which result, on the one hand, in the people's increased affection and, on the other, in Saul's increased hatred of David (v. 29).

19:1–7: Saul schemes to kill David, but Jonathan intercedes and restores David to Saul's favor. The suspicion has been voiced by a number of scholars that this passage is a briefer version of the same story told in chap. 20. It should be noted, however, that the two passages have different endings. Here Jonathan brings about a reconciliation between David and Saul. In chap. 20, however, the breach between the two is made final.

19:8–10: David successfully leads Saul's troops in battle and Saul, enraged at David's victories, tries to impale him with his spear. This is perhaps a version of the same incident reported in 18:10–11. Saul's spear functioned as a kind of scepter of authority which would explain why it was within easy reach even when Saul was in his own house, presumably the fortified structure which archeolgists have unearthed in Gibeah (see 22:6).

19:11–17: Saul attempts to kill David in David's own house, but Michal cooperates in a ruse by which David escapes. This story takes on a more realistic flavor if we understand "that night" in v. 11 to be David's and Michal's wedding night. It then is seen as a continuation of 18:20–29. In other words, Saul has grown so insanely jealous of David that he tries to kill him at a time and place in which he would be most vulnerable, in bed with his new bride. Michal's cooperation, however, simply underscores the extent to which even Saul's own family has gone over to David (but see 2 Sam 6:20–23).

19:18–24: David flees to Samuel. Saul sends three consecutive teams of men to kill David, but they fall under the ecstatic spell of Samuel and his school of prophets. Finally, Saul himself goes with the same result. This seems to have been an anecdote which, when circulating independently, served as an explanation of the saying recorded in v. 24 about Saul. This is a different explanation, of course, from the one in 10:10–13.

Nine stories have thus been strung together by the final editors of 1 Samuel with little effort on their part to smooth out interruptions to the narrative flow which these stories introduce or to reconcile differences among them. As a result, seams where they have been sewn together are easily identified.

No less obvious are the reasons why these vignettes have been included. On a literary and human-interest level, they form the bridge between the introduction of David into the life of Saul's court and the final break between the two men which will be consummated with Saul's death and David's first moves to consolidate the kingdom under himself.

On a theological level, the purpose of these stories is (to repeat) to remind the reader that, in abandoning Saul, God did not abandon his people. Rather, he raised up one greater than Saul to lead the people and to be to them the representative of Israel's true king, the Lord himself.

Because these various narratives, although numerous, repeat much the same theological and psychological themes, there is perhaps not as much preaching material as one might first assume. But one may wish to consider the following two themes:

"There Is No Fury ..." based on 18:11. We have previously (see comments on 12:1–25) discussed a sermon which explores the power of that love which responds to rejection with still more love. This verse is a study in the opposite, a study in the corrosive effects of hatred and jealousy. One may speculate endlessly over the relationship between Saul's rejection by Samuel and his growing emotional instability. The deuteronomistic historians certainly understood the first of these as the cause and the second as its effect. However, there may also have been a kind of psychological "feedback loop" by which the two tragic facts reinforced one another, that is, that the more surly Saul's disposition grew, the more convinced Samuel and the people became that God had turned away from Saul. This, in turn, caused Saul's moods to become even blacker. There is ample evidence in this extended section that Saul's despair pushed him further into terrible acts of duplicity. In 18:17–19 he offers his daughter as bait to get David into battle (and, he hoped, into a grave), but then, at the last minute, withdraws the offer. In 18:22 he surreptitiously hatches a similar scheme. In 19:11 he plants his assassins to murder his new son-in-law on what was perhaps David's wedding night. The contrast to Saul's evil temper is the kindly disposition toward David of both Jonathan (19:1–7) and Michal (19:11–17). As a result, Jonathan is remembered with affection by subsequent generations of Hebrews, and perhaps Michal would have been also, if it had not been for the incident of 2 Sam 6:16–23.

Modern parallels to the tragedy of Saul's decline abound. On a personal level, there are examples in every congregation and parish of those who have allowed some personal frustration to eat away at their hearts until they have made life unbearable for themselves and for everyone around them (contrast the comments about Hannah's reaction to rejection in 1 Sam 1). The cause of their deep disappointment has become a kind of self-fulfilling prophecy: the person has been declared "unfit" in some particular way, and he/she now seems hell-bent to prove that judgment correct. The minister needs only to supply names and faces of persons he or she knows. But there is also an important corporate dimension in which these dynamics of self-damnation operate. If there is a group of people in society who are told in some manner that they do not measure up, they may soon begin to believe that judgment and may more and more act it out. The problem of high teenage (especially minority) unemployment in certain metropolitan areas is a case in point. It is not

by accident that that social phenomenon frequently goes
hand-in-glove with high rates of crime. And we seem to have
gone beyond the point where unemployment "causes"
crime—they both feed off each other. All of which reminds us
of the importance which a society must place upon equal access among its citizens to education, jobs, and the like.

Another and, if possible, even more knotty question is
posed in 18:10: "Does God Really Cause Evil?" A turning
point in the narrative of 1 Samuel is signaled by the comment in 1 Sam 16:14 where a "spirit from the Lord" is replaced by "an evil spirit" in Saul's life. In 18:10 it is "an evil
spirit from God" (as in 16:23 and 19:9). This is not the place
to engage in a discussion of the OT views concerning evil, but
it should be noted that while the OT is ambiguous in its
views on the origin of evil (compare 2 Sam 24:1 with 1 Chron
21:1), it does affirm that some evil deeds seem to have their
origin "outside" the person who commits them, that there is
a kind of supra-human evil at work in our world. (I believe,
with many scholars, that the above reference to the "evil
spirit from God" is an effort to say this in an age before a
concept of a "Satan" [Hebrew: "Adversary"] had become
current.) However this may be, the average reader of 1 Samuel may be pardoned if he/she comes away from the text convinced that God does (or causes to be done) evil in our world.
A sermon might be crafted which would speak to this dilemma by (1) pointing out that the OT actually speaks of evil in
many symbols, of which the above are one group, and (2)
drawing attention to the language Jesus used about God in
such places as John 3:16 and 14:9. One would then want to
go on to discuss that, whatever one makes of the biblical portrait of Satan, there do seem to be certain evil forces un-
leashed *in* our world which are not *of* our world. Some would
(rightly, I believe) characterize the holocaust in such terms,
or the threat of nuclear war. No one who believes that he/she
has encountered God in the person of Jesus Christ would en-
tertain for a moment the belief that God was the author of
such evils. That person would, however, doubtless believe
that, just as God resists all such evils, so should God's people.
That resistance may (indeed, *must*) take the form of (1) working with others to prevent or overthrow such evil and (2)
praying that the goodness and love of God will prevail in our

time. The writers of the OT were aware that, in discussing the relationship between God and evil, they stood before a mystery. That mystery is not resolved for us, but in Jesus Christ we see God's basic hostility toward those forces which destroy life and joy and we hear his call to join him in opposing them.

The Friendship of David and Jonathan (20:1–42)

The close companionship between David and Jonathan, Saul's eldest son, has been referred to before (18:1–5, 19:1–7), but the most extensive treatment of this theme is found in chap. 20. The story occupies an important place in the narrative flow of 1 Samuel because it marks David's final effort to come to terms with Saul. David's flight in 20:42 is his "crossing of the Rubicon," the final turning of his back on Saul's court. From that point on he is to be hunted as an outlaw and is to live the life of a bedouin raider, a condition which will continue until Saul's death.

There are a number of interesting features to this pericope. One of these is the picture of David's place in the life of Saul's court. He appears here as more than a mere retainer. Because of his marriage to Michal (18:20–29) and because of his victories in the field (18:5, 19:8), he has been elevated to the level of those who eat at the king's own table. This select group may have included a number of individuals, but we know of only two others, Jonathan and Abner, Saul's commander-in-chief, who were so chosen (20:25, see 2 Sam 9:13, 2 Kings 25:29). David's "fall" from this rarified social atmosphere to the life of an outcast was a dramatic touch which would not have been lost to ancient readers of this tale.

The story also tells us something of David's moral character, namely, that he was not above telling a lie to achieve his purposes. To be sure, the falsehood in this instance is a minor one, that he intended to spend the festival of the New Moon with his people in Bethlehem. Even so, a lie at this time was not necessary. David could have accomplished his purpose, to discover Saul's attitude toward him, by some more forthright means. Thus his stratagem on this occasion is an early clue toward some of the moral flaws which will later bring tragedy to himself and to those around him.

One element, however, which is not in this story is that

the relationship between David and Jonathan assumed the nature of a homosexual liaison. The allegation that the two men had such a relationship is made from time to time (primarily on the basis of 2 Sam 1:26), but it should be stressed that there is no real suggestion of this in the text. If the deuteronomistic historians had suspected something of this nature, they would not have been the least bit bashful about reporting and condemning it, just as they demonstrate no reticence in reporting and condemning David's adultery with Bathsheba and his complicity in the death of Uriah the Hittite (2 Sam 12). On the contrary, the love of David and Jonathan is the deep affection which is often experienced by comrades-in-arms.

Of considerable importance to the structure of this passage, and perhaps some clue to those circles where it circulated before it assumed its present place in 1 Samuel, is the dynamics of the David-Jonathan relationship. Clearly, David is the dominant figure and Jonathan is one who, by making himself available to help carry out David's purposes, ingratiates David to him and, it should be stressed, to his descendants. V. 4 depicts Jonathan as one who is simply waiting for David to tell him what to do, while the brief passage, vs. 14–17 (see v. 42), is straightforward in declaring that David is under special obligation to Jonathan's descendants because of this loyalty. (Even Saul senses this "special relationship," which explains his outburst in vs. 30–34.) From a structural standpoint, this helps pave the way for the account of David's kindness to lame Mephibosheth (2 Sam 4:4; 9:9–13, see 1 Chron 8:34 which states that his name was actually Meribbaal), but it also suggests that this story may have been used often by Mephibosheth and those around him during the time of David's bloody purges of Saul's descendants in order to remind David's officers that they were immune from the king's wrath (see 2 Sam 21:7).

Perhaps the most curious feature of this narrative is the ruse which David and Jonathan decide upon as a means for communicating to David the state of Saul's mind (vs. 20–22). When Jonathan tells the young boy to search for the arrows in a manner which will tell the hiding David that Saul is ready to kill him (vs. 37), he then sends the boy away while David comes out of hiding in order that he and David may bid one another farewell. The question, of course, is why was the ruse necessary? Why didn't Jonathan simply go out to David and say what had happened? There is nothing in the story which helps us to an answer.

Theologically, this passage has little to add to what the final editors of 1 Samuel have said over several chapters: God has chosen David to fill the void in Israel's life caused by the growing impotence of King Saul. Even Saul's own family has shown sympathies toward the young Judean, and it is this aspect of the drama which the present chapter portrays in extended detail. It is therefore not surprising that, when this passage has been mined for material for preaching, much interest has been usually shown in its human qualities: Jonathan's willingness to die for his friend, David's willingness to make amends with the jealous Saul, the poisonous hatred which is destroying Saul and his kingdom. There is much illustrative material here for the preacher to use, many "windows" into the human condition. Yet it should not be forgotten that here, as throughout the deuteronomistic history, the most important word is a word concerning God and his saving activity in the life of his people.

There is one important point in chap. 20 where the psychology of the narrative is integrated into the authors' theology, and here a sermon might be written around the theme "Two's a Party, Three's a Godly Crowd." In v. 8 David reminds Jonathan that the relationship between the two friends involves the Lord himself: "you (Jonathan) have brought your servant into a covenant of the Lord" is a literal rendering of the Hebrew. Moreover, David prefaces that statement with a request for Jonathan's continuing faithfulness by invoking the Hebrew term (hesed) which is often used in the OT to refer to the steady, unflagging covenant love of God (RSV's "deal kindly" does not quite capture the force of the Hebrew). These statements in v. 8 should be compared with similar affirmations in v. 23 ("the Lord is between you and me forever") and v. 42 ("the Lord shall be between me and you, and between my descendants and your descendants, forever"). Taken together these texts provide an insight into one of the ways the OT views human relationships, namely, that God is a third party to all human intercourse, and that he has a stake in the manner in which we

deal with one another. If we violate a relationship, we sin; if
we affirm and support the well-being of others, we do God's
will. It is in this spirit that Joseph refuses the advances of
Potiphar's wife ("How can I do this great wickedness and sin
against God?" Gen 39:9), and it is in this spirit that the author of Psalm 51, by tradition the adulterer David, understands his transgression against Bathsheba as an act of
iniquity against God (Ps 51:4). (The force of this verse is the
same whether one agrees with the tradition of Davidic authorship or not.) In terms of our own lives the biblical insight
is extremely important, having weighty implications for
such questions as the nature of marriage and family life, the
manner in which we function in the political arena, the
shape of our economic structures, to name but a few. And so,
a sermon on the theme of God's involvement in our relationships might take the following form: (1) The preacher might
begin with a "case study" which illustrates how one person
may violate the dignity and well-being of another. Sadly,
there is no shortage of such examples, such as two persons of
my acquaintance who are now in divorce court. He is a successful physician, she a faithful wife who worked hard after
their marriage to put him through medical school. They are
the parents of three young children. During recent years he
has become more and more immersed in his work and has
had less and less time and attention to give to his family. Finally, about a year ago, he announced that he was going to
seek a divorce. There is no other woman in his life (which is
unusual in such cases). He just wants to be free to "do his
thing." He is well paid for his services as a physician, but she
will have to live off of an allowance which barely meets her
and her children's needs. After the youngest child is 21, she
will receive no alimony at all.

   (2) The preacher may next contrast this pattern of behavior with a discussion similar to the one above concerning the
biblical view of human relationships. The OT does not suggest that such an attitude toward human relationships neces-
sarily results in "sweetness and light." The turmoil of
David's own life should tell us that. But it does affirm that
when we consider God to be a third party in our interactions
with others, the quality of those interactions may, indeed *will*
be changed.

(3) The preacher is now free to go in one of two directions, or perhaps, both directions at once. There is a personal, individual side to this whole matter, of course, and this
may be pursued with the idea of challenging one's hearers
into building their own relationships in the light of God's
presence. (Beware here of being sentimental, on the one
hand, or judgmental, on the other.) But there is also a corpo-
rate/legal/social dimension to many of our tragedies in
human relationships. To refer back to the "case study"
above, what is the moral justification for laws relating to the
status of women which (as is true in many states) place them
at a financial and social disadvantage in the divorce courts?
Why could not the wife in this example claim a larger and
more permanent portion of her husband's future earnings on
the basis of her contribution to his medical education (he
might not even *be* a physician today if she had not financed
that education)? One will want to study the laws in his/her
own state, in order to discuss the problem intelligently. If we
consider God to be a third party to marriage, many mar-
riages would prove more durable and those which could not
be saved might have a more merciful termination. (Note:
Sermons which deal with divorce and the laws relating to
divorce are difficult to preach because the preacher must
avoid (1) being judgmental, (2) being a pollyanna, and (3)
causing anyone in the congregation to feel "on the spot." Yet,
as every minister/priest knows, there are few areas of greater
pastoral—therefore homiletic—concern.)

Saul Murders the Priests of Nob (21:1—22:23)

A rather lengthy passage now describes a deed of Saul
which is easily the most heinous transgression which the OT
charges against Israel's first king, surpassing even those of-
fenses for which he is being divested of his office (chaps. 13,
15). As the story now stands in 1 Samuel it is interrupted by
references to the activities of David, now a fugitive from
Saul's anger (21:10–22:5). Originally, however, the account
of David's visit to Nob and the consequent murder of the
priests who lived there formed a single narrative.

The debacle at Ebenezer (1 Sam 4) had resulted not only
in a serious military defeat for Israel which included the loss
of the Ark of the Covenant, but also in the death of Eli and his

two sons, Hophni and Phinehas (1 Sam 4:17–18). What is
more, the chief Hebrew sanctuary at Shiloh also seems to
have been destroyed at this time (Jer 7:12, 26:9). Yet not all
of Eli's priestly clan was lost. At least two generations have
passed and we now find a grandson of Phinehas, Ahimelech,
presiding over the sanctuary of Nob, a Hebrew community
located a mile or so north of the Jebusite settlement of Jerusalem. (The Ahijah mentioned in 14:3 may be a brother of
Ahimelech or, more likely, another name for the same person.) The presumption is that the ancestors of these Eli
priests fled to Nob following the destruction (or decline) of
Shiloh where the family has ministered since.

Nob, some two miles south of Saul's citadel at Gibeah,
becomes David's first stop on his flight toward the wilderness of the Negev. Accompanied by a few of his companions
from Saul's army who have chosen to cast their lot with him
(and who are to become the nucleus of his personal army),
David approaches Ahimelech for food. The priest is at first
suspicious because David is unaccompanied by his usual
fighting force (v. 1), but, when assured that he is on a mission
for the king (a lie) and that his men are sexually and ritually
clean (possibly another lie), Ahimelech gives them the sacred
bread of the Presence (see Lev 24:5–9). He also turns over to
him the sword of Goliath, which had found its way to Nob by
a means of which we are ignorant. David and his men, now
refreshed, continue toward the south.

The story, which breaks off at 21:10, resumes at 22:6. It
is not clear in what sense David has been "discovered" (v. 6).
It is likely that some element in the original story was
dropped out with the introduction of the material in
21:10–22:5. This element probably had to do with David's
flight, so that Saul's "discovery" is that David has left
Gibeah with a party of armed men, that he is, in effect, in
open rebellion against Saul's authority. Saul's questioning of
his men (vs. 7–8) would then be understood as an effort to
find out where David had gone.

An Edomite mercenary named Dŏeg, who had left
Gibeah with David's band, but who had turned back with
their departure from Nob, steps forward to supply Saul
with the information he seeks (vs. 9–10). After interrogating
Ahimelech who, incidentally, conducts himself with great

integrity (vs. 14–15), Saul orders the murder of all of the priests of Nob, together with the members of their families. Even their livestock are killed (v. 19). Again it is Doeg (and presumably the contingent of men whom he commanded, perhaps also Edomites) who does the king's bidding. None of the native Hebrew warriors, although accustomed to slaughter and bloodshed, is willing to commit so great a sacrilege.

Still, however, the house of Eli is not quite obliterated. A son of Ahimelech, Abiathar, escapes and makes his way to David in the south. He is to remain at David's side for the rest of his (David's) life, and the allegiance to the young Judean of this representative of the Eli priesthood (Samuel's sympathy toward David was probably widely known by now, as well) helped to swell the tide of David's popular support.

There are several fascinating ingredients within this narrative: Again (as in chap. 20), there is David's willingness to deceive to attain his ends. (Jesus' affirmation in Matt 12:3–8 of David's action here should not be interpreted as a condoning of David's deceit, but rather as a statement to the effect that even holy things—sacramental bread, the Sabbath—are intended to meet human need.) Also the portrait of the growing desperation of King Saul which would lead him to commit such a monstrous deed is an important means by which we are reminded that Saul's days are numbered. Not only is human life taken on a wholesale scale, but the sacredness of the cult is desecrated since the victims were priests of God. (It is interesting that there is no explicit condemnation of Saul here, as in chaps. 13 and 15, although the crime, even in ancient Israel, would have been considered extremely serious.)

It may be, in fact, that the greatest usefulness of this entire narrative for purposes of preaching lies in the dynamics of human personality which it depicts. There is no strong theological statement here, other than that general principle which characterizes this entire part of 1 Samuel, namely, that God has chosen David to replace Saul. But we do have subtle reminders that sin is universal: "good" David lies, "evil" Saul murders. And we are also reminded that, in the case of David, at least, God sometimes uses even the sinful deeds of men and women to accomplish his purposes (see Gen 50:20).

The three digressions which interrupt this larger story are of some importance in understanding David's situation at this point in his life. 21:10–15 is an account of an attempt by David to find shelter from Saul's anger among the Philistines of Gath, a theme which will recur again. This passage is notable in that it once more repeats the song concerning David's military prowess (v. 11, see 18:7, 29:5). It is also interesting that the Philistines are described as knowing that David is "king of the land," but seem ignorant of the fact that this is the conqueror of Gath's mighty champion, Goliath.

22:1–2 gives important information about the nature of David's growing band of freebooters. Not only has he been joined by those defecters from Saul's army who have followed him south, but outcasts and dissidents generally, as well as members of his own family, come to swell his ranks once the news of his whereabouts leaks out. David's subsequent campaigns of plunder (e.g., 23:5) may be explained in part as arising out of the necessity to feed his men and to give them something to occupy their time.

A final digression in 22:3–5 notes that, in the face of Saul's anger, David sends his mother and father to live under the protection of the king of Moab. This may be an echo of the tradition of David's Moabite blood (Ruth 4:22).

For purposes of preaching, the most suggestive text within this extended passage may be 22:14–15 which could serve as the basis of a sermon on the theme "Whatever Happened to Honor?" Ahimelech's response to King Saul is the one example of truth and personal integrity in this whole tale of flight by misrepresentation (David) and of vengeful murder (Saul). To be sure, the reason for Ahimelech's innocent response may lie partly in the fact that he is perhaps still in the dark concerning the complete breakdown of the relationship between Saul and David. Yet he was probably a perceptive person and would have quickly sensed the depth and cause of Saul's anger. The fact that he makes no effort to provide the king with a self-serving answer, but tells him the unadorned truth, is very courageous. The anger and emotional instability of Saul was such that he would likely have killed

Ahimelech and his priests regardless of Ahimelech's response, so the point to this episode is not "tell the truth and you may die for it," but "there are some men and women around whose integrity is such that they will tell the truth even in the face of great personal loss."

A possible outline for a sermon on this text might be: (1) Truth is a curiously potent commodity in the social intercourse of human beings. Because it is the one essential element in human communication we may generally assume that almost everything we hear from others is true. Imagine for a moment what it would be like to live in a world in which we, like Alice in *Through the Looking Glass*, had to assume that most human communication was false! Even the most rudimentary interpersonal functions would come to a halt and life would be reduced to the level of the Stone Age or worse. Because of this general assumption of truth in our dealings with one another, we are made particularly vulnerable to truth's counterfeit, the lie. If more people lied more often we might be more sceptical about human communication generally. But he/she who perverts the truth and speaks (or performs) a falsehood is cashing in on the fact that we all generally anticipate the truth from each other.

(2) Consequently, the power of the lie is enormous, and this is perhaps best illustrated when some falsehood is uncovered by a revelation of the truth. In our community a man who claims to have been an eye witness to a sensational murder of more than sixty years ago has stepped forward to say that the convicted perpetrator (who was taken from jail and lynched by a mob) was innocent. This is because he claims to have seen the man who was the star witness for the prosecution holding the body of the victim shortly after the murder took place. Some members of our community have been relieved to know that the truth is (presumably) finally "out" and the name of the innocent party can at least be cleared. But others are angry that the reputed eye witness did not come forward years before. The preacher can doubtless think of examples within his/her own community of the devastating power of the lie. Or he/she may turn to such a notorious example as the Nazi propaganda machine which skillfully blended lies and truths so that the two were often indistinguishable. (Remember, of course, that even democratic gov-

ernments have not always told the truth to their own people
or to others!) When falsehoods are perpetrated, the very basis
of meaningful human relationships is threatened or
destroyed.

(3) The biblical concern for truthtelling is connected
with the holiness of God and with God's concern for the well-
being of the human individual and community. The Ninth
Commandment has a social orientation, while Jesus' statement in Matt 5:33–37 seems to imply that if one must invoke
the name of God to authenticate one's speech, both human
and divine relationships are threatened. Many of our
forebearers and (thank God!) many of our contemporaries
have connected the telling of the truth to a quality called
"honor." One told the truth because to fail to do so violated
the sense of his/her own worth. Ahimelech told the truth
even in the moment of his death because to fail to do so
would have been to inflict upon himself a far greater suffering than that which was about to be inflicted by Saul. He
would have been dishonored in the eyes of God and in his
own eyes. The fact that there have been such people in the
past and still are such persons today helps to preserve the
ability of the human family to communicate with one another and gives us hope for the future of honor.

David's Outlaw Days Begin (23:1–24:22)

David's break with Saul is now complete. Although the
young Judean will again demonstrate his good will toward
the king, Saul's state of mind and spirit, in addition to his
obvious deficiencies of ability in comparison to those of
David, have rendered impossible the likelihood that Saul
will ever accept his brilliant subject back into the life of the
court. As is to be expected, the material which was available
to the deuteronomistic historians in constructing this portion of the narrative of David's life consisted primarily of
brief popular tales concerning David's exploits in the south
as an outlaw. This is to be contrasted with the literarily more
sophisticated material pertaining to David's later life, material, especially the Succession Narrative, which was the
product of skilled court annalists (see Introduction). The result is that the story of David's outlaw life in the wilderness
of southern Judah has an anecdotal flavor, for it is apparent

that the deuteronomists strung their material together in such a manner as to give it chronological coherence, but without adding much in the way of editorial comment or embellishment. (This is similar to the fashion in which, as previously noted, chaps. 18–19 have been constructed.)

Let us take a brief look at each of the individual units in chaps. 23 and 24. 23:1–5 is the summary account of the rescue by David and his men of the town of Keilah from a Philistine attack. David had little reason to love the Philistines, in spite of his previous attempt to find refuge in Gath (21:10–15) and his subsequent service as a Philistine vassal (chap. 27). Yet this action should not be thought of as a pure act of patriotism on David's part, to be compared to Saul's relief of the citizens of Jabesh (11:1–15). As noted above, David's primary motive for attacking the Philistines at Keilah was probably to provide provisions and employment for the large group of freebooters and dissidents who had attached themselves to him. And just as David was no Robin Hood, his followers were by no means "merry men." As v. 3 suggests, they were often insubordinate and difficult to control.

23:6–14 confirms the above picture of the nature of David's military operations at this point in his life. Far from being grateful to David and his "army," the citizens of Keilah are willing to betray them into the hand of the king (v. 12) when the news comes of the approach of Saul and his troops. The goods which David's men "liberated" were apparently not only those of the Philistines, but those of the townspeople as well. The mention here (v. 6) of Abiathar is interesting (see the comments on 21:1–22:23). The manner in which the Lord's will was ascertained by means of the ephod is uncertain, but may have involved some form of lot casting.

23:15–18 gives a notice of the visit of Jonathan to David in the Wilderness of Ziph, the arid region southeast of Keilah to which David had been forced to flee as a result of the approach of Saul's army. The implication is that Jonathan was a member of the fighting force which had come to capture David, but that he slipped away from the main body of Saul's army (not unlike his action in 14:1) and secretly came to David in order to renew their friendship.

23:19–29 reveals something of the desperate situation of

poor King Saul. His main enemy is, as has been the case all along, the Philistines, who still covet control of the central hill country. Only the presence of Saul and his army have kept them at bay, but now the intelligence that Saul is in the south chasing his rival encourages them to attack. We are not told the location of the Philistine action, but presumably it is farther north, in the Benjamin or Ephraim hills. And so a frustrated Saul, who has almost snared David in his net (v. 26), is suddenly called away to deal with this fresh menace. No doubt David, and the deuteronomists after him, considered this salvation to be an act of God. Also of interest in this anecdote is the fact that the people of the region, like the citizens of Keilah, were willing to hand David over to Saul (vs. 19–20). David's sense of social and political isolation at this point must have been very great indeed.

24:1–22 is the narrative of the manner in which David spared the life of Saul in the Wilderness of Engedi, the inhospitable region along the western shore of the Dead Sea to which David has now retreated. The nature of David's behavior is similar to the incident recorded in chap. 26, and the two stories may be, as some scholars suspect, variant accounts of the same incident. Of equal interest to the account of David's cutting off of the tail of Saul's robe (vs. 1–7) are the speeches of David (vs. 8–15) and of Saul (vs. 16–22) which follow. Some analysts of this literature have felt that this exchange of remarks seems contrived and artificial, in the nature of editorial additions to the story. Saul's remarks seem particularly vulnerable to this charge, since they not only contradict almost everything else that we know of his attitude toward David, but also his subsequent hostile actions. (Vs. 21–22 suggest that they may have originally been some sort of *apologia* by Saul's descendants, not unlike 20:14–15.) David's remarks, however, seem more in character. This was the man, it must be remembered, who could be capable of the most astonishing acts with respect to other people (see 2 Sam 23:13–17), and whose respect for the cultic institutions of Israel, including the office of king, was very great.

The interest of the preacher may be drawn to a pair of passages as material for sermons. 23:6–13 (esp. v. 9) suggests the theme "On Fetching the Ephod." The ephod was a cultic apparatus of some sort, whose exact nature is not known (a

good Bible dictionary will be helpful here), but it is clear that
it was a device which, among other things, was considered
capable of divining the will of God. David's reliance upon the
mechanism may seem superstitious to modern readers of the
Bible, but the deuteronomistic editors of 1 and 2 Samuel
were not as concerned about *how* David opened himself to
the word of God as *that* he did. As we have discussed before
(see Introduction), the final editors of 1 and 2 Samuel seem
convinced that David succeeded Saul because he was open to
God's presence in his life and the life of the nation, even to
the point of accepting God's judgment after his notorious affair with Bathsheba (2 Sam 12:13). Saul, on the other hand,
is portrayed as rarely, if ever, seeking God or of responding
to God's presence when the Deity sought Saul. Here David,
finding himself in a precarious position, turns to God to as-
certain not only Saul's intentions and those of the citizens of
Keilah, but in a larger sense, to determine the will of God for
his life. This action should be compared to the later desperate effort of Saul, in a similar predicament, to seek the help
of a witch (chap. 28). One would not want to push the point
too far and thus fall into the trap of portraying prayer as a
twentieth century fetish, but there is a strong word to be said
about the importance to life of prayer and of openness to
God. There is no assurance that such openness results in
wealth, or longevity, or any of those other qualities by which
"success" is often measured. But the theological promise of 1
& 2 Samuel seems to be that such openness results in a deep-
ened sensitivity to God's will for all human life and in a
heightened awareness of one's place in that will. David's no-
tions of the nature of prayer were much different than our
own, but they obviously played an important role in his life.
There is no reason to believe that prayer should play less of a
role in our lives.

Another theme might be that of "The Quality of Mercy"
based on 24:8–15. To be forgiving toward one's enemies is
not a virtue which comes easily to a man or woman. Even
David could demonstrate sharp vengefulness on occasion (cf.
25:13, 21–22), and the natural response of most of us in the
face of some injury or slight is similar. The story of God's
dealing with his people, however, reveals that one of the in-
fluences that God exercises upon humankind is that of moral

restraint and forgiveness. The supreme example of this is Jesus' own attitude on the cross (Luke 23:34), the same Jesus, of course, who had reminded his disciples that human forgiveness and divine mercy are intertwined (Matt 6:12). David is willing to place his controversy with Saul in God's hands (v. 15) and he therefore suppresses whatever urges he may have felt to do hurt to the king. Consider the countless situations in contemporary life where harm to the body and spirit of others could be avoided if men and women exercised more mercy and less judgment.

David's Hard Times in the Wilderness (25:1–28:2)

The three chapters 25–27 offer several "windows" into the nature of David's life as the chief of a band of roving warriors, insights which tend to confirm the suggestion of the preceeding section that these were unpleasant and grueling times in David's life and that those who came into contact with his men were not always the better for the experience.

The unit begins with an unadorned announcement of the death and burial of Samuel (25:1a). The only temporal reference is the word "now" which we may perhaps understand as meaning sometime during David's flight to the south. From a literary standpoint, Samuel has not been a principal character since the introduction of David into the drama (the last reference to him was in 19:24), thus the brief notice given here is a means of confirming what the reader already knows: that Samuel has made his final contribution to Israel's life (but see 28:14–19).

The balance of chap. 25 (vs. 1b–44) is devoted to a description of the manner in which David claimed as his bride a woman of the south, Abigail. Those who were responsible for first circulating and preserving this story were probably interested in it primarily from a genealogical point of view (see 2 Sam 3:3). The deuteronomistic editors then told the tale in such a manner as to highlight its theological message: namely, that even in the wilderness of the Negev the Lord was guiding the affairs of David (note esp. vs. 30–35). And now, to both of these reasons for interest in the story must be added our own fascination for what it tells us about the conditions under which David and his men lived during the time of their exile.

In regard to these conditions, several things stand out. To begin with, David and his people had no specific geographical location to call their own, but were a roaming body of several hundred men and, presumably, their dependents (see 27:2) who were forced to live off the land. In the southern wilderness they were, in fact, one such group among many (cf. 30:1–3), for here there was no established order and no effective means of enforcing those conventions which prevailed in more established communities in the hill country to the north and in the Philistine areas to the west. Therefore, those peaceful citizens who did inhabit the region and who sent their livestock out to graze at the various oases under the watchful eyes of hired shepherds would normally be glad to encounter non-violent nomads, who, instead of plundering their herds, helped to care for them. Nabal's ingratitude (25:10–11) seems out of place on these grounds, although he could not be blamed if he saw in David's proposal more than a hint of extortion. With respect to the "heroine" of the story, Abigail stands out as only slightly more admirable than her husband. Her concern for Nabal's life and property is minimal compared with her interest in David (vs. 24–28), and her praise of David (vs. 26–31), which may seem self-serving to some (v. 31), is another means by which our attention is drawn back to the central thread which runs through this entire section of 1 Samuel: David is the true anointed of the Lord (note her emphasis on David's "house," that is, his dynasty, in v. 28).

The chapter ends with a note about Ahinoam, who is to become the mother of David's son, Amnon (2 Sam 3:2), and with another to the effect that Saul had given Michal another husband, perhaps as punishment to both her and David because of the incident related in 19:11–17.

A second larger unit within this section, 26:1–25, is another story of David's restraint when the vengeful Saul falls into his hands. Many of the literary and theological characteristics of this story are closely akin to 24:1–22, so much so that, as stated above, many scholars consider them to be two versions of the same incident. Be that as it may, it is important to notice that in chaps. 24–26 the deuteronomistic editors have given us three consecutive major tales which highlight the moral restraint of David.

Of specific interest in 26:1–25: In seizing Saul's spear (v. 12), David was taking more than the king's weapon. He was also confiscating the symbol of royal authority. Also, vs. 19–20 give a quaint insight into the "territorial" manner in which Israel once viewed her God. In being driven from his homeland, David is being denied his "share in the heritage of the Lord" (vs. 19). And if he is killed here, the Lord will not avenge his death because this ground is "away from the presence of the Lord" (v. 20).

In spite of these important spiritual considerations and in spite of Saul's conciliatory remarks (26:21–24—which David apparently does not believe), David now volunteers for service as a vassal of the Philistine king of Gath, Achish: 27:1–28:2. (We are left in ignorance concerning why the objection raised in 21:11 is not raised here, but cf. 29:4–11.) This is an important step in David's career for, although it is a move which may have seemed traitorous to some, David for the first time claims his own territory, the southern oasis of Ziklag. This will ultimately prove to be the "springboard" from which he will launch his operations to claim, first, Judah, then all Israel as his kingdom. (For an interesting modern parallel, note the historical relationship of the Channel Islands to the remainder of the United Kingdom.) This relationship is, for the moment, satisfactory to both David and Achish: to David because he now possesses his own oasis where the creature comforts of his followers may be more easily supplied and to Achish because he counts on David to secure his flanks to the south and east against the nomadic raiders and against settlers from Judah and their allies, the Jerahmeelites and the Kenites (v. 10). But notice David's duplicity in this latter regard (vs. 11–12).

This larger section reminds us, again to borrow Shakespeare's words, that "The web of our life is a mingled yarn, good and ill together." The picture of David which emerges is one of sharp contrasts. Adored by his family and his followers and hated by his enemies, he can be merciful and restrained (26:9–12) or bloodthirsty and vengeful (25:13). Although he will not kill Saul, he is not above striking an alliance with Israel's mortal enemies in order to achieve his goals. David knows the value of truth, yet he is willing to lie to the priests of God as well as to the Philistine ruler.

If one wishes to employ these contrasts within David as material for a sermon entitled "At Odds With Ourselves," one may compare 26:9 (in which David affirms the sanctity of Saul's life) and 28:1–2 (where David promises loyalty to Achish, although his promise threatens and brings him into bloody conflict with Saul). One of the most insightful stories in English literature is Robert Louis Stevenson's *The Strange Case of Dr. Jekyll and Mr. Hyde*. We usually think of this as science fiction and place it in the same category as other nineteenth century fare such as *Frankenstein* and *Twenty Thousand Leagues Under the Sea*. However, just as Jules Verne was ahead of his time in describing a world of technology which was not to dawn for a hundred years or more, so Stevenson was ahead of his time in understanding the complex manner in which the human psyche is often at war with itself. Written before the impact of Freud, *Jekyll and Hyde* described in narrative form something of the same emotional and psychological conflict which Freud was to identify using the tools of psychoanalysis.

Internal conflicts play a part in every human life. For some those conflicts are paralyzing, and help of a specialized nature is required. We have almost gotten to the point where psychoanalysis does not carry the social stigma that it did a few years ago. In fact, in some circles it is the "in thing" to see an analysis on a regular basis. Yet everyone remembers what happened a few years ago when a candidate for Vice President revealed that he had submitted to psychoanalysis.

For most people, inner conflicts are not severe enough to be paralyzing, but are present nonetheless. They were certainly present in David's life, as the examples above illustrate. In a sense, therefore, David is Everyman. He is you and I, good and evil intertwined. If his virtues seem expansive, so do his faults. From a theological perspective, the point is not that God will deliver us from our conflicts. (David is delivered from the conflict between 26:9 and 28:1–3 by a kind of *deus ex machina* [chap. 29]. One should be careful not to imply to one's hearers that such a deliverance can be expected from their conflicts.) The theological point is that God does not rely on "plaster saints" to achieve his purposes. He depends upon us, warts and all. And there is a sense in which our inner conflicts must be endured or resolved as well as possible, while we busy ourselves with doing God's work in this world, as we come to understand that work through prayer, the reading of Scripture, and participation in the life of the Christian community.

Another theme within this larger section could be "Lord, I'm Innocent," based on 26:17–20. We in the Christian tradition have generally laid a great deal of stress in corporate worship as well as in individual devotional life upon the importance of confession. It has been pointed out that no relationship with God can be healthy without the free admission of our sin and such passages as Ps 51 and the Lord's Prayer (esp. Matt 6:12) have been relied upon to provide the models for our prayers of confession. Without question, there is great theological and psychological value to this tradition, one whose place needs to be strengthened and reaffirmed in every manner possible. But we sometimes forget that the biblical tradition also gives important room to the complement to the prayer of confession, that is, the affirmation of one's innocence. This affirmation is often expressed in time of calamity or tragedy when the faithful person (or community) knows that he/she has done nothing to deserve the present suffering and throws him/herself upon the mercy of God. Job is a classical biblical example of a person who protests his innocence and who will not accept the simplistic solutions to his predicament offered by his friends ("you are suffering, therefore you must have sinned"; see Job 11:13–15). Rather, he doggedly asserts his own innocence (Job 9:13–24, compare Jesus' statement in John 9:3). A number of the Psalms of Lament strike this same chord (see Ps 7:3–5; 27:11–12, for example). It might not be wise for us to institute into our liturgy of worship an "Affirmation of Innocence" to stand alongside our "Confession of Sin." (Or perhaps it would be wise under certain circumstances. The psalms referred to above suggest that such an act of worship held a place within the cult of ancient Israel.) In any event, David's statement in 26:17–20 is an important text in which he insists on his basic innocence before Saul and before God. He also casts himself upon the mercy of Saul and of God to redress this wrong. The preacher may wish to use this text to explore with his/her hearers the importance of affirming one's worth before God and within the context of the social fabric in which we live.

(See David's comments in 26:23-24 which are a part of this same dynamic.)

Saul's Tragic Death (28:3—31:13)

The climax to the larger unit which began in chap. 16 and which describes David's ascendancy over Saul is now reached with this account of Saul's death at Mount Gilboa. The story of Saul's death (chaps. 28, 31), however, has been interrupted by two narratives which trace the activities of David during the final Philistine campaign against Saul. In one of these (chap. 29) we are advised, by means of a kind of literary "flashback," that almost before the Philistine offensive is underway, David is dismissed from the service of King Achish. In the other (chap. 30) we follow David back to the south and see him avenge an attack upon his base in Ziklag. All of this material, which originally came from different sources, has been skillfully woven together by the deuteronomistic editors in such a way that we are allowed to watch the movements of Saul and David as this part of the larger story of 1 & 2 Samuel rushes toward its conclusion.

The tragic quality of Saul's end did not consist, for those who were responsible for the material in 1 Samuel, simply in the fact of his death, but primarily in its manner. 28:3-25 poignantly illustrates this by showing how those impetuous qualities which had once served Saul so well (11:1-15), but which had later begun to work to his detriment (18:10-11, 22:6-19), were now about to destroy Israel's first king. Driven to desperation by his inability to annihilate the Philistine menace, by his repeated failure to crush the rebels led by David, and by what must have been his own awareness of his precarious state of mind, Saul resorts to magic in order to save himself. His very choice of this tactic is itself an insight into the contradictory and self-destructive mood which now gripped him, for the Saul who travels by night to seek the aid of the witch of Endor (28:8-14) is the same Saul who not long before had outlawed such practices (v. 3). His disguise betrays to the reader the magnitude of his fall from grace. Ostensibly it is to prevent Saul's identification by the Philistines near whose sentries he must pass (Endor was just to the north of Shunem, the encampment of the Philistine army—v.4) and to prevent his recognition by the witch herself who, when she does realize that she has entertained the king, fears for her life (v. 21). However, Saul's disguise also serves the theological purpose of reminding us that, in spiritual and psychological terms, this is not the same man whom we met in chaps. 9–11. The bright, energetic Saul of those days, anointed by the Lord's priest and endowed with the Lord's *charisma*, has now become this shell of a king upon whom the Lord has turned his back. That the Samuel who anointed him should also deliver his sentence of death (vs. 15–19) is a means, from the standpoint of the manner in which the story is told, of emphasizing the same point. There are few sadder portraits in the OT than this one of King Saul.

One military note is of interest. The scene of this action carries us much farther to the north than we have thus far been in 1 Samuel, for the Philistine army has now penetrated the Plain of Jezreel (or Esdraelon), the valley which runs southeast from Mount Carmel and which links the coast with the Jordan Valley. The precise reason for the presence of the Philistine army here, so far from their usual base of operations, is a matter of some conjecture. Perhaps they were attempting to cut Saul off from his supporters in the region of the Sea of Galilee, or perhaps they intended to march down the Jordan Valley and to attack Saul's stronghold in the Benjamin hills from the rear. Whatever their reason for being here, Saul has come north to meet them and, in spite of the biblical evaluation of Israel's first king, you and I cannot help but admire his courage.

Saul's death is now a certainty, but those who were responsible for the final shape of 1 Samuel prevail upon us to pause momentarily to look in upon David. The action of 29:1–11 seems to have occurred prior to that of chap. 28. The reason for concluding this is that the Philistine army, which is encamped in Shunem in 28:4, is only as far north as Aphek in 29:1. This spot seems to have been a favorite point of muster for the Philistines (see 4:1) and may even have served as the sight of a permanent Philistine garrison. The implication seems to be that the army is first constituted at Aphek (contingents would have been contributed from the various Philistine city-states) and is then marched northward into the Jezreel Plain. It is therefore on the occasion of this initial muster that certain Philistine leaders question the loyalty of

David and force Achish to dismiss him from the Philistine ranks (29:3–11).

The passage raises intriguing and unanswerable questions about the loyalties of David. Would he actually have fought with his Philistine overlord Achish against his fellow Hebrews once the battle was joined? Did he hope to contribute to the defeat of Saul in the expectation that the Philistines would set him on Israel's throne thereafter? Or did he plan, as some of the Philistines feared, to act as a "fifth column" in the Philistine army and to fall upon his pretended allies from the rear in the heat of the battle? We shall never know, for the objections lodged by the Philistines to his presence in their army prevented him from carrying out whatever scheme was in his mind.

Two notes of interest: The Hebrew word in 29:4 which many English versions render "adversary" (so RSV) is the same as that which in other places is translated "Satan." Also notice in 29:5 the third occurrence of the, by now, familiar jingle (cf. 18:7, 21:11).

30:1–31 chronicles the affairs of David upon his return to the south from the Philistine campaign. In the absence of his 600 warriors, a group of Amalekite bedouins, who have no love for David (see 27:8), overrun Ziklag and, after burning the settlement, carry away all of the women and children (presumably to be used or sold as slaves). David's reaction is as swift as it is typical in that he quickly avenges the dishonor done him by his enemies and uses booty gained to enrich himself and his friends. This latter action, in fact, tells us something about David's strategy for making allies. He not only insists that the spoils of war be shared with the 200 warriors who had been too exhausted to participate in the fight (30:21–25), but he also sends articles of value to friendly people throughout the Negev (some of whom had probably also been victims of the Amalekites). By this means David ensured the loyalty of his followers and cemented relationships with his neighbors.

In theological terms, David is portrayed in 30:1–31 as one who is blessed by God and who is aware of his dependence upon the Lord. His seeking of the will of the Lord before the battle (v. 7) and his credit to the Lord for the victory (v. 23) make that evident and, once again, underscore the essential theological proclamation of this part of 1 Samuel: David is the Lord's anointed to whom he is giving the kingdom.

31:1–31 recounts Saul's death and brings 1 Samuel to a close. The narrative resumes the story broken off at 28:25 with the simple, unadorned notice of the Hebrew defeat by the Philistines (31:1). The ignominy with which 1 Samuel characterizes the death of Saul is portrayed in the method of his death (he is the only major figure in the OT to die by suicide) and in the desecration of his body and those of his sons by the Philistines (vs. 8–13). With the report of this information the prophecy of Samuel delivered as far back as 13:14 has now been realized and Saul's rule as well as his life is now at an end.

There is a final word of grace, however. When the people of Jabesh, whom Saul had delivered in his (to the best of our knowledge) first military campaign as king (11:1–15), hear of their benefactor's death and of the desecration of the bodies, they risk their own lives to retrieve the remains of Saul and his sons in order that they may be given honorable burials (vs. 11–13). 1 Samuel ends by informing us that they then fasted seven days, the only community in all of Israel whose formal sorrow for Saul has been recorded.

In preaching from chaps. 28–31, one's emphasis should be, as was that of the deuteronomistic historians, on the grace of God that raised up David to deliver his people. Illustrations of grace abound, not only the grace of God, but also instances of human grace, as in David's gracious treatment of his Egyptian prisoner (30:11–15), his generosity toward his friends (30:21–31), and the care of the Jabeshites for the bodies of Saul and his sons (31:8–13).

A sermon on the theme of grace might focus on 30:11–15 and receive the title "God's Love, Our Opportunity" (or "Lord of Love, Lord of Life"). The anecdotes which tell of David's adventures during the climax of his outlaw period have unquestionably preserved a great deal of the character of the man. As these stories circulated orally, they were probably intended to portray, among other things, the means by which David generated such loyalty in others that they were willing to do anything for his cause. 30:11–15 and 30:21–31 agree upon an essential theme about David, that is, that his generosity and magnanimity were often expressed at a time when other, less charismatic leaders would have given vent to outrage, revenge, or indifference. And these acts of large-heartedness galvanized the affections of the people to him in quite remarkable ways. As the deuteronomistic historians re-tell these episodes, however, they are held up against the background of that grace of God for Israel which raised up David. In other words, David's acts of grace towards others are seen in our texts not simply as expressions of his charac-ter, but as statements about the nature of Israel's God.

Therefore, a sermon on this theme might be built around three propositions: (1) God's love is contagious. True, it is not irresistibly contagious, for countless persons through the ages have responded to it with apathy or worse. Neverthe-less, it does have a quality of infection about it. It possesses the ability to reduplicate itself in many hearts (see 1 John 4:19). The history of the Church is filled with stories of men and women who have lived sacrificial lives because they have been touched by God's love. The preacher might wish to relate here such a story as that of St. Martin of Tours and the beggar. He/she could probably find many examples of this kind of self-giving love in his/her own community.

(2) The love of men and women is contagious, as well (again, not irresistibly so). Everyone knows the power of self-giving love in the task of raising children (beware of indul-gent permissiveness, however—see 1 Kings 1:6). But that same power is evident in other dimensions of life. "A soft an-swer turns away wrath" (Prov 15:1), yet in reality it also does more. A generous and magnanimous spirit kindles the affec-tions of others so that they often respond in trust and loyalty. David is an important biblical example of this (and here the preacher could discuss the above texts in some detail), and his life is important not just as an insight into the way in which human beings interact, but as a statement about God.

(3) When the people of God live sacrificial lives, it is not because we "choose" to do so, but because, in a sense, we "have" to. The analogy of the parent and the child is helpful, again. In homes where psychic and spiritual health prevails, the parent does not have to decide, upon arising each morn-ing, whether he/she will love the child that day. That love is a "given," it is an inner impulse which has become a part of

the fabric of the parent's person. And those commitments which must be renewed each day (to be more patient with spilled milk, to be more firm about muddy shoes on the carpet, etc.) are made out of the "givenness" of love. In the Christian life the "given" is the love of God in Jesus Christ which "compels" us into a concern for others. Because of the contagious nature of Christ's love, we live that love, making daily decisions concerning how it may best be expressed.

Another kind of grace is expressed in 28:20–25 (to back up a bit) which tells of "The Best Witch in the Bible." The strongly negative view of the Bible toward such things as witchcraft, sorcery, astrology, and the like is evidenced by a number of texts (see a good Bible dictionary). Even King Saul, in spite of whatever spiritual flaws he may have had, has banished the practitioners of these arts from Israel (v. 3). But when his prayers to the Lord are of no avail, he turns to a witch in desperation in order to discover the outcome of the impending battle with the Philistines. (One may wish to ponder the pitiful portrait of Saul here, a portrait which may evoke a certain sympathy for Israel's first king.) Although he comes disguised, the woman learns his true identity and, when Saul finally faints out of weakness and fear, she tends to his physical needs. She has placed her own life in jeopardy be admitting him to her home (v. 21), but she will not allow him to leave until she has ministered to him. And the food which she serves him is not some ancient equivalent of a quickie "TV dinner." Rather she kills the fatted calf (v. 24) and bakes unleavened bread, and both Saul and his entourage eat their fill. In reading this passage, one thinks of the woman in Matt 26:6–13 who was blessed for honoring Jesus with a simple act of hospitality as he drew near the cross. Jesus' words in Matt 25 also ring in our ears. By means of this curious episode, the wicked Witch of Endor has become a heroine of God (notice that the Magi of Matt 2, themselves practitioners of forbidden arts, in this instance astrology, also become heroes of God). She is thus not only an example for all men and women everywhere, but is also a symbol of the basic redeemability in the eyes of God of anyone.

2 SAMUEL

David Consolidates
His Kingdom
(2 Samuel 1:1—10:19)

As stated in the Introduction, the Books of Samuel form one continuous literary unit with the Books of Kings. However, with the division of this material in ancient times into four extended sections, it seemed logical to introduce the first major break following the narrative of the death of Saul. The new section, our 2 Samuel, is therefore devoted entirely to the story of David's turbulent rule over the Hebrew people. Before David may call Saul's kingdom his own, however, the remnant of Saul's supporters must be suppressed, the hearts of the population as a whole won over to David's cause, and Israel's borders made secure against hostile neighbors. The account of these achievements is contained in the first ten chapters of 2 Samuel.

David: King of Judah (1:1—2:7)

The brief section which culminates in David's acclamation as king of Judah begins with a story of the manner in which David learns of the death of Saul in 1:1–16. Some scholars have concluded that this material was originally composed by a person who did not know 1 Sam 31, for several details surrounding the death of Saul seem contradictory in the two narratives. The most important is that in 1 Sam 31:4 Saul is described as a suicide, while in 2 Sam 1:10 the Amalekite boasts that he killed Saul upon the latter's urgent request. The two passages may have had different origins, to be sure, but it may also be true that the Amalekite presented David with a "cock-and-bull" story in an effort to win David's favor for having dispatched his rival. If so, the man was surely shocked at David's response (1:15).

This execution of the Amalekite is the first of several instances in which David is quick to put distance between himself and others who lay hands upon Saul and his family. We will examine other examples of this reaction by David in time. It should be noted here, however, that while we are not in a position to question David's sincerity, such a posture could have been calculated to earn him the favor of those remnants of the population who were still loyal to Saul's house and whose allegiance David needed if he was ever to unite the kingdom under himself. What is more, David, who had just slaughtered an entire Amalekite raiding party (1 Sam 30:1–20), would have had few qualms of conscience over one more Amalekite death. Therefore, in David's execution of the man we have one of several examples of a convergence between the will of God (as David interprets it—1:16) and his own political designs.

A second unit within this section consists of a lament in vs. 17–27 by David in which he expresses his and the nation's grief over the death of Saul and Jonathan (interestingly, no mention is made of the other two sons of Saul who died with him, Abinadab and Malchishua—1 Sam 31:2). In spirit as well as in form the poem is a traditional Hebrew lament, or *kinah*, whose simple and plaintive beauty make of it a fitting tribute to Israel's first king and his eldest son. We usually think of the Psalms as that part of the OT which most profoundly attests David's skill as songsmith, but this beautiful lament presents itself as an example of David's creative genius, as well. (It should be noted, however, that not all scholars accept the poem's Davidic authorship.) It is not surprising that David would speak of Jonathan in phrases such as this poem contains, but the positive portrait of Saul given here is largely unexpected, in view of David's troubles with him and also in view of the opinion of Saul in the eyes of the deuteronomistic historians (who might easily have decided not to include this lament). There is not the slightest hint of the breach between David and Saul nor a single negative innuendo cast in the dead king's direction. Perhaps David genuinely felt such grief because of his view of the office of the "Lord's anointed" (vs. 14, 16). Or perhaps with Saul now out of the way David could simply afford to be magnanimous. Or perhaps David speaks well of Saul as a means of appealing to Saul's followers. Here, as at many points in his career, David's true motives remain a mystery.

As a climax to this section, we are told that David is acclaimed king over Judah and we are informed of his first act thereafter (2:1–7.) From very early in Israel's life in Palestine a rift is noticeable between the northern and southern tribes, notably between Judah and the others. The reasons for this tension are unclear, but it will ultimately result, of course, in that schism which tears the Hebrew kingdom apart (1 Kings 12:16–20). For now, however, Judah's independence of her sister tribes consists in the fact that she is willing to accept her own native son as king, in spite of the fact that a son of Saul who claims Israel's throne is very much alive (2:8–11). David has now moved his base of operations from Ziklag to Hebron, still far to the south, but nearer to both his home in Bethlehem and to the central hill country which is a center of sympathy for the house of Saul (and a region still under Philistine control). To the oasis of Ziklag is thus added the somewhat more densely populated country in the south as the terriory now under David's influence. The Philistines, who still regard David as their vassal, are either ignorant of the action of the Hebron assembly or simply assume that David is acting in their own interests, for they make no effort to restrain him.

David's first act as king of Judah is to send a message of affirmation to the community of Jabesh for their loyalty to Saul (vs. 4b–7). The reader of these verses may wish to assume that David is sowing seeds of friendship among Saul's followers which he someday hopes to harvest.

In theological terms, the section 1:1–2:7 represents a partial fulfillment of that promise contained in 1 Sam 16:6–13. There God through his spokesman Samuel promised Israel a new king and, although much struggle lies ahead, the first steps toward that goal have now been taken. If he is not king of the entire nation, he is at least sovereign over Judah. In terms of human personality, however, we find the section to be a fascinating character study. David presents himself as one genuinely grieved over Saul, yet the steps he takes to express that grief dovetail very nicely into his own political schemes. In this passage we are thus able to see that David had a singular ability to further his own ends, yet to do so in a manner in which he also appeared to be serving some higher moral or spiritual cause.

For purposes of the crafting of sermons, one may wish to use this section to raise the question "Why Do We Do What We Do?" In other words, how do we come to terms with our own motives? In *Murder in the Cathedral*, T. S. Eliot causes the archbishop (who is tempted to use martyrdom as a weapon against his enemy, the king) to say

> The last temptation is the greatest treason:
> To do the right deed for the wrong reason.

Yet who of us can entirely know our own motives? And is it necessary to have "pure" motives before we can do the will of God? Certainly, Jesus had much to say about the importance of being "pure in heart" (Matt 5:8), and there is a great deal in his teaching, especially in the Sermon on the Mount, to the effect that what goes on in the "interior" of an individual is of more consequence than many of our expressions of faith which "show" (see esp. Matt 6). Yet the suggestion of 2 Sam 1:1–2:7 seems to be that we, like David, may sometimes have mixed motives, in fact, may often not realize just what all of our motives are (just as we cannot discover all of David's true motives in this passage). Nevertheless, mastering our motives as best we can, we commit ourselves to the doing of the will of God, as best we understand that will. Beyond that, we trust in the power of God's Spirit to compensate for our own deficiencies (note David's reliance on God in 2:1).

Another theme, this one suggested by 1:25–26, might be "The Joys of Having (and *Being*) Friends." These verses form the climax to the David-Jonathan friendship (although its implications for Jonathan's son, Mephibosheth, are to continue for some time), and we have already discussed our view that they do not, as is sometimes supposed, suggest a homo-sexual liaison between David and Jonathan (see comments on 1 Sam 20). Other friendships are hinted at in the OT (Abraham-Melchizedek, Jeremiah-Baruch), but none is de-scribed so fully as this.

V. 26 is an expression of joy in the midst of an otherwise melancholy lament. It is as if, even in the midst of his sorrow, David delights in the memories of his and Jonathan's times together. (Note the contrast between the adjective "dis-tressed" [so RSV] in v. 26 and "pleasant," "wonderful" in the same verse.) We doubtless do not have all of the details con-cerning David's and Jonathan's mutual exploits, but enough is known to enable us to understand Jonathan as both a brave warrior and an unselfish friend (how easy it would have been for him to be jealous of David for, after all, he stood to lose the most from David's increasing popularity!) and to see David as one who, in this relationship, embraced Jonathan as a comrade-in-arms to be trusted and honored, and not as a potential rival to be eliminated.

Here the preacher may look into his/her own life, or into the lives of other persons whom he/she knows well, and iden-tify those moments when friends have meant a great deal: during college, or boot camp, or in time of illness or grief. One fact which often emerges from such recollections is the reciprocity which is necessary to all lasting friendships: *Having* a friend means *being* a friend. (Some of the loneliest and most unhappy individuals whom I have known are persons who would gladly receive from others, but have never learned to give of themselves.) David and Jonathan gave to each other their loyalty and trust in a context which would have elicited from less expansive souls only suspicion and spite. Their friendship stands, therefore, as a model for all human relationships.

David: King of Israel (2:8–5:5)

The account of David's acclamation as king by the elders of Judah at Hebron is followed almost immediately by a no-tice that the survivors among Saul's family and his close sup-porters have taken measures to insure the continuation of Saul's dynasty in the north (2:8–9). The purpose of this entire section, 2:8–5:5, is to narrate that chain of events by which the intentions of the Saulites are frustrated and David is received as king over a united Israel.

The passage 2:8-11 describes the location of the court of Saul's son Ishbosheth in the transjordanian community of Mahanaim (v. 8), which is a clue to the fact that the central hill country to the west of the Jordan, the normal center of Saulite loyalty, was now under firm Philistine control. (Ishbosheth, which means "man of shame," is a scribal alteration to avoid the use of the man's real name, Eshbaal, "Baal exists"–see 1 Chron 8:33.) Therefore, the very location of the court, away from the centers of Hebrew life, suggests that Ishbosheth's grasp upon his father's kingdom is precarious from the beginning.

As one might expect, trouble soon breaks out between the warriors of David and those loyal to Saul's son. The story of one such encounter in 2:12-32 not only provides us with an example of the armed tension which existed between the two Hebrew camps during David's years in Hebron (3:1 suggests many such encounters as this one), but it also sets the stage for the rivalry between David's chief warrior, Joab, and his counterpart in the Saulite army, Abner. Several features of this incident are interesting. The location of the combat (Gibeon is in the territory of Saul's tribe, Benjamin) implies that the young men of David may have gone prowling in the hopes of encountering some of Saul's people, while the verb "to play" hints that a kind of mock or representational combat got out of hand and soon became the real thing. In any event, David's warriors won the day (v. 17), and the surviving members of the Saulite patrol were soon in retreat. We cannot help but be sympathetic to Abner when he is finally forced to kill Asahel (v. 23), for to have failed to have done so would have meant his own death at the hands of Joab's determined brother. Only the appearance of a band of Benjaminites, loyal to Saul's cause, saves Abner, who then leads his weary, defeated troops back across the Jordan to Mahanaim. Two incidental notes: this episode marks the first mention of Joab (v. 13) in the OT material pertaining to David. Also, the Pool of Gibeon (v. 13) is still in existence.

A brief section, 3:1-5, takes note of the "long war" between the followers of Saul and those of David (v. 1), and then matches a list of David's sons born at Hebron with their mothers (vs. 2–5). We have already been provided with the information that the duration of David's rule as King of Judah in Hebron was seven and a half years (2:11).

The single event which proves decisive in ending this protracted period of civil conflict is the defection and murder of Abner, as described in 3:6–39. (If the information in 2:10 that Ishbosheth ruled two years is correct, that would determine the length of the "long war," but that datum is difficult to harmonize with the seven and a half years of 2:11.) Saul's old warrior may have seen the handwriting on the wall and realized that the momentum of history was with David (note 3:1b). Certainly his defection was encouraged by his dispute with Ishbosheth over a woman of Saul's harem, Rizpah. It will be remembered that the harem was the property of the crown, and Abner's union with Rizpah (v. 7) was quite correctly judged by Ishbosheth as an act of treason (note Absalom's violation of David's harem "in broad daylight" in 2 Sam 16:21–23 as another act of political insurrection). Ishbosheth's logical, angry response is all Abner needs to declare his intention of joining David (vs. 9–10).

Another example of the importance of the harem is found in David's initial reaction when he receives the intelligence that Abner wishes to defect. David demands the return to him of Saul's daughter Michal. David had won Michal only after a "herculean" effort (1 Sam 18:20–29—note David's comment in 2 Sam 3:14), following which she had saved his life (1 Sam 19:11–17). Saul had subsequently given her to another man after David had fled to the south (1 Sam 25:44). David now insists upon her return to him, not simply as an act of love, although that may have been involved (Paltiel certainly seems to have loved her, v. 16), but because he was concerned to claim what belonged to him. If he was king, then no other man had a right to any member of the royal harem. The fact that she was Saul's daughter might also prove helpful in winning the allegiance of those Hebrews who still honored the memory of Israel's first king.

For his part, Abner, before actually going over to David's camp, seems to have made a small journey through country loyal to Saul to win popular support for the effort to place David on the throne of all Israel (vs. 17–19). The tragic events which unfold when Abner presents himself to David is another of those instances in which the true motives of David may not be entirely spelled out. Several things seem certain. First, Abner comes to David in good faith, believing that he will be accepted in David's camp on the basis of David's assurances (v. 13). David receives the Saulite leader cordially, but at a time when the hot-blooded Joab is out of the camp with his raiding party (v. 22). David could not have been ignorant of their absence, nor of the bad blood between them over the death of Asahel. When Joab returns and berates David for his hospitality to their enemy (vs. 24–25), David's silence is thunderous! There is recorded not a single word from David's mouth in the way of an effort to cool Joab's temper. We are not surprised, and David would not have been surprised, when Joab calls Abner back and coldly murders him as he steps foot inside the Hebron gate (v. 27).

David protests, of course, but one suspects that his heart is not in it. The same David who killed the Amalekite who reported that he had slain King Saul (2 Sam 1:15), and who will order the execution of those who are about to slay Ishbosheth (2 Sam 4:9–12—it must be remembered that Ishbosheth did not, in David's eyes, come under the rubric of "the Lord's anointed," as did King Saul) is satisfied to reprimand Joab, after having protested his own innocence (vs. 28–29), and to proclaim a period of public mourning preceding the funeral. It would be an injustice to read too much into this story, but the narrative as it stands certainly leaves many unanswered questions about David's role in the affair. There is no doubt, however, about the public reaction to all of this, especially among the followers of the house of Saul. The people admire David (v. 36), but perhaps do not notice that, while maintaining a respectful distance from the event, David has gained the removal of a powerful adversary.

With Abner's defection and death there is now no strong personality to defend the weak Ishbosheth, who is soon murdered by two opportunists who bring the bloody head of Saul's son to David at Hebron, as we read in 4:1–12. They obviously expect a reward, perhaps on the basis of David's mild response to the murder of Abner. They are killed, however, and their bodies are desecrated, while Ishbosheth's head is buried with honor beside his former commander (v. 12). The "long war" is over and the Hebrews can, at last, turn from killing one another to the task of ridding the land of the well entrenched Philistines.

As a natural act, therefore, David is proclaimed king by the leaders of the tribes which have been loyal to Saul (5:1–5). Traveling to Hebron, the "elders of Israel" seal this transfer of their loyalties by means of a covenant ratified in the presence of God (v. 3). For the first time since his anointing as king by Samuel in 1 Sam 16, David rules indeed over all the tribes.

For purposes of preaching one text which stands out is 2:26 which suggests a sermon on the topic "Of Black Holes and Warfare." Astronomers tell us that there are certain objects in space whose matter is so dense and whose consequent gravitational field is so strong that anything trapped in that field is pulled inexorably into the object. These so-called "Black Holes" (the name, of course, comes from the fact that not even light can escape their magnetic fields and that they thus appear through a telescope as dark areas) were popularized by a Walt Disney movie, but they are also a phenomenon which is under close scrutiny by professional astronomers.

2:26 is a poignant statement by a beleaguered Abner that human warfare is a kind of psychological "Black Hole." Once the sword draws blood it is very difficult to put an end to the killing and the suffering. Abner's only choices in vs. 18–23 were to kill Asahel or to be killed by him. And now Joab, enraged by his brother's death, is forcing the same horrible dilemma upon Abner. Abner somehow senses that this will prove to be only the beginning to a wider and more prolonged conflict (the "long war" of 3:1) which will not end until much of Israel's finest manhood is slain.

Much of history certainly underscores the accuracy of Abner's remarks. World War I is an especially graphic example of how a group of powerful nations blundered their way into an unplanned and unexpected bloodletting the most lasting effect of which has perhaps been the rise to political power (by means of the Russian Revolution) of international Communism. And as horrible as were World Wars I and II, the present age makes their weapons seem like pop-guns. As I write, the radio announcer has just finished describing an exchange of very hostile remarks between Moscow and Washington over the likelihood of nuclear war. In hearing such comments one is seized by the horrible sensation that humankind is very possibly being sucked, slowly, surely sucked, into the Black Hole of nuclear holocaust. It is the feeling that, as in 1914, we are blindly and foolishly groping our way into a Pit from which there is no return. It is the terror that Abner's fears in 2:26 are coming true in a manner which he never dreamed, even in his worst nightmares.

The threat from nuclear warfare is the single most urgent moral question on the world's agenda, and therefore upon the church's agenda. It transcends party politics and all sectarian concerns. And the preacher is in a unique position to speak a biblical word to this question. That word, of course, is peace, a peace achieved by an aggressive effort on the part of western nations to be defensively strong, on the one hand, and on the other, to seek ways to reduce international tensions through arms reduction talks and by means of mediation in areas of open conflict. Some of the preacher's hearers may be in key positions to influence national policy in such matters. And all of us as citizens may make our concerns known to those who wield political power.

Another sermon might be crafted on the theme of "Crocodile Tears," relying upon 3:26-39. As one reads 1 and 2 Samuel, one is continually fascinated by the varieties of human conduct exemplified by David. Many of these are of sterling quality, of course, and provide models for the living of our own lives before God. Many others, however, reveal David's feet of clay. In theological terms, David's flaws are understood by the deuteronomistic historians as evidence of God's grace in the face of human sinfulness. David's weak behavior in the matter of Abner's murder falls into this latter category. His reaction in 3:26-39 does not ring true, and we suspect that Joab must have known beforehand of David's "soft" attitude toward his (Joab's) hatred for Abner. David's weakness results not only in Abner's murder, but probably in that of Ishbosheth as well, since Rechab and Baanah (chap. 4) were probably encouraged by events at Hebron.

And so David's moral weakness has its price, yet that weakness is not sufficient to frustrate the grace of God. It is a sinful David, but David nonetheless whom God uses as the instrument by which the kingdom is secured.

And so something like the following outline emerges:
(1) Men and women of faith are also men and women of sin.
(2) While God rejects our sin (which often causes hurt to ourselves and/or to others), his Spirit is still at work to redeem and use us.
(3) Here we stand before the mystery of God's love. If we take that mystery seriously, we will be motivated to greater acts of self-giving, and the sin within us will be chastened by the Spirit (within us) of God.

David: King of Jerusalem (5:6—6:23)

There are three principal geographical territories now under David's personal rule: Ziklag in the far south, Judah, and Israel. Each area has come to David at a different time and in a somewhat different manner and, as yet, they have not been melded together into a political unit, in spite of the obviously close ties between Judah and her sister tribes to the north. David now strikes a bold blow which seems intended not so much to add to the territory under his personal dominion (although it has this effect) as to provide a new focus for the nation's political and spiritual experience. David captures the Jebusite community of Jerusalem and (1) makes it into the center of his people's political life by building there a royal palace, and (2) he centers there the worship of God by transporting to the city the Ark of the Covenant. Even before David is able to complete this action, however, there is a strong negative response from the Philistines.

The section begins with a brief account of the capture of Jerusalem by David and his armed men in 5:6–10. The narrative is remarkable for its terseness in view of the enormous importance to Israel's history of the event which it describes. Not only so, but even the little information which is supplied seems to have been garbled before reaching its present literary form, for we simply do not understand all that is implied in the references to "the blind and the lame" in vs. 6 and 8. It is evident that the deuteronomistic historians had very skimpy materials with which to work in describing this crucial event in David's life. However, it does seem true, as has often been observed, that David's design upon Jerusalem had to do with the fact that, as a Jebusite city, it belonged to no one tribe and would therefore make an ideal hub around which to galvanize the life of the kingdom (cf. the creation of the District of Columbia by America's Founding Fathers).

Vs. 11–16 report that David lost no time in moving the royal court to Jerusalem. He builds there a palace with the help of the Phoenician king, Hiram of Tyre, and enlarges his household. In theological terms, this short notice contains the key verse for the entire section, v. 12, to which we will later return.

In vs. 17–25 the Philistines, who up to this point in David's career have continued to regard him as their vassal and who have looked the other way in the face of his growing success, now become alarmed. When they realize that David is no longer the obedient inferior (indeed, was he ever?) but has large political and military ambitions of his own, they attack him. It would only have been a matter of time before David had clashed with the Philistines under any circumstances, given their dominant position in the hill country and their military control over the Hebrew settlements there. However, this contest, to judge by the geographical references, seems to have been an attempt by the Philistines to dislodge David from his new royal capital. Having been repulsed on their first attempt (vs. 17–21), they return again with what is presumably an even larger force, only to be turned back once more (vs. 22–25). Although we are not specifically told that such is the case, it may be that these were very massive battles, especially the second encounter, for never again do we hear of a serious Philistine threat to David's kingdom. And so that menace which had led to the people's original call for a monarch (1 Sam 8:4–5) and which had plagued Saul all of his days as king, ultimately to cause his death, is now dispelled by David in the early days of his rule over Judah–Israel. Is it any wonder that the people adored him and reserved for him a niche in their hearts which outlasted even the kingdom which he established? With respect to the second battle, one suspects that there is more than meets the eye in the reference to the sound of marching in the tops of the balsam trees (v. 24), that is, that there was once a meaning here which has now been lost to us. In any event, however, David used this sound as a signal to know when to attack the Philistine army.

Having established Jerusalem as the political center of

his nation and successfully defended it against military assault David now proceeds to make of it the focus of the nation's spiritual life (6:1–23). This he does by bringing to it the Ark of the Covenant which has been neglected by the Hebrew tribes since the days early in the life of Samuel when it was the center of a series of tumultuous events (1 Sam 4–6). The incident involving the death of Uzzah (6:6–11) strikes the same discordant note in the mind of the modern reader as did the stories of the Ark's effect upon the Philistines (1 Sam 5) and upon the citizens of Beth Shemesh (1 Sam 6:19–20). As there, however, one should not allow this vestige of a cruder age to obscure important words about the ancient Hebrew concept of the holiness of God (see the comments on 1 Sam 4:1b–7:2).

David's ecstatic dancing before the Ark (v. 14) may be related to prophetic ecstacy as described in 1 Sam 10:9–13. Also, his wearing of the ephod and the report of his offering of sacrifices (v. 17) suggest that he was assuming priestly prerogatives, precisely the sin for which Saul had been condemned by Samuel some time before (1 Sam 13:8–15). Michal is repelled by David's behavior, ostensibly because he danced nude (v. 20). Although it is not stated, one wonders if her resentment may not also be related to the fact that David "gets by" with a deed for which her father was roundly condemned.

At the end of the section 5:6–6:23 the core of David's kingdom has been established. Although his borders will presently be extended, Judah–Israel, now incorporating David's original base at Ziklag and with Jerusalem as its center, is at this time brought firmly into a political union whose center of gravity is the king himself. Space does not allow us to discuss in detail the enormous consequences for the people's life of the dramatic change this represents from those days when the centripetal force which held together the loose confederation of tribes was the worship of God as presided over by such figures as Eli and Samuel. Nor is it possible to do more than simply mention the fact that this union achieved by David is a fragile and temporary one, an amalgam which will not survive the death of his son Solomon (1 Kings 12). We may simply take note of David's accomplishment and salute him for it.

Yet, it was not a feat of David alone. As mentioned above,

the central verse of this section is 5:12 which not only credits David's successes to the Lord, but reminds us that David understood that the guiding hand of the Lord was upon him. This statement is, of course, consistent with the principal theological motif which shapes this part of the deuteronomic history and, moreover, it relates to such passages as 5:24 where David received divine aid in his struggle to preserve his new capital. Therefore, "The Sound in the Balsam Trees" becomes a symbol for the energetic presence of the Lord in human life, for to David the sound in the tops of the trees meant that the Lord was "on the march." Note Jesus' statement in John 3:8 that the Spirit of God is like a wind which "blows where it wills." Unfortunately, not every enthusiasm or *charisma* is divine, but part of the challenge (and adventure) of the Christian life is to "hear the sound of marching" and to join the pilgrimage. William Carey and Albert Schweitzer are two examples, one recent, the other not so recent, of those who heard and went. Do we listen today? Are we prepared to join the "pilgrim throng?"

Another possible sermon theme is that of "Celebrating God," based on 6:5. All of chap. 6 is permeated with a feeling of great joy over God's presence in Israel's life and his goodness to David. The theme of merry making which is struck in 6:5 is repeated in 6:19 (where a feast of the people is described) and in 6:21 (in which David insists upon the appropriateness of his joy in the face of Michal's anger). The fact that the joyous mood is interrupted by the incident involving Uzzah (vs. 6–11) and by Michal's bitterness (vs. 16, 20) should not be allowed to obscure the essentially celebrative quality of this chapter. The spontaneity of David's and the people's joy, perhaps even its charismatic flavor (compare 6:5 with 1 Sam 10:5) is unmistakable. The preacher may wish to use this text to discuss the place of celebration in the public worship of God. On the one hand, unrestrained joy may easily lapse into a kind of emotional orgy. I remember a congregation of "holy rollers" (as we called them) who had a storefront church not far from our neighborhood when I was a boy. On Wednesday nights my friends and I would occasionally go down and peep between the curtains which hung in the windows in order to watch them carry on in what we considered to be a most ridiculous manner. On the other hand, however, it may be said that there are too many of our "mainline" churches where worship is so formal and controlled that genuine expressions of emotion are almost impossible. It may be that many of our black churches have done the best job of combining reverence and spontaneity, the strong "amens" from the pews and the lilting rhythms of the spirituals expressing both joy and sobriety at the same time. Each worshipping community must decide for itself questions having to do with the proper forms of worship. But 2 Sam 6 certainly speaks a word for the place of joy.

Another interesting text in this chapter is 6:8 which opens the possibility of a sermon on "When We Are Angry At God." The very thought of hostile emotions directed at God is offensive to some persons in our churches. Such a feeling suggests to them that one is in rebellion against or defiance of God. And yet there are several instances in the Bible in which important characters, persons whom we usually consider to be spokespersons *for* God, vent their displeasure at what God has done in their lives. David is the example here, but there are also Job (Job 3:3–10) and Jeremiah (Jer 20:14–18, compare Jer 20:7) who both curse God indirectly by cursing the day of their birth. Even Jesus reproaches God from the cross (Matt 27:46, from Psalm 22:1). It is a psychological fact that there are times when we are *mad* at God, and those are usually times when the injustices of life press upon us. Often we try to conceal our anger by denying it, but that device frequently results in simply more emotional stress. And so it may be that, like David and Jesus, we are better off in moments of tragedy and crisis by admitting our anger at God. For such a moment of truth often has a strange way of opening up the heart of the suffering person to even greater experiences of God's grace. Martin Luther, who admitted that the elaborate penitential system of the medieval church drove him to hate God, used that admission as a door through which to enter into a new life. In part, at least, that was the spark behind the Reformation.

David Extends His Borders (7:1—10:19)

It is a curious feature of the deuteronomistic history that, in describing the life and times of David, so little information should be furnished about the extensive middle years of his reign, the period in which he was extending Israel's boundaries from Egypt in the south to the Euphrates in the northeast. This is to be contrasted with the extensive detail we have relating to David's early years and that relating to the struggle among his sons to succeed him. Concerning the great wars of territorial expansion we have only the brief notices in 2 Sam 8 and 10, together with a few other miscellaneous references (e.g., 11:1) as material out of which to reconstruct this important period in the life of the Hebrew kingdom. Undoubtedly more detailed information was not available to the deuteronomistic historians (for reasons we do not know) or they would have preserved it. It has been suggested, however, that the military operations which led to the creation of David's expansive empire, the largest the ancient Hebrew state was to know, may be broken down into three phases: (1) the consolidation of Judah–Israel into a unified monarchy, including the incorporation of non-Hebrew elements who lived west of the Jordan (certain peoples of the south such as the Kenites, Jerahmeelites, etc., in addition to such others as the Jebusites of Jerusalem); (2) the conquest of the desert kingdoms (Edom, Ammon, Moab) just east of the Jordan; and (3) the annexation of the strong Aramean power centers (Damascus, Zobah, Toi) to the northeast. The present section is devoted to a fleeting glimpse into the nature of operations during the second and third of these phases.

The section begins with a narrative designed to answer the question: "Why did David not build a great Jerusalem Temple?" in 7:1–29. The reason is a theological one, namely, that the old ways in which Israel worshipped its God were quite sufficient, and God, who did not ask for a cedar house in the days of the judges, is not asking for one now (v. 7). Interestingly enough, Nathan's speech seems to be a denunciation of the very idea of having a temple at all and the suspicion is aroused that there may have been a silent minority who were later to view Solomon's successful efforts in this direction with alarm. The prophet proceeds to turn the question so that, by means of a word play on "house" (v. 11), he looks forward to the establishment by God of David's "house" (i.e., his family "dynasty") instead of the other way around. This chapter thus becomes a keystone for that important theology which characterized the outlook of the Jerusalem community right up to NT times, a theology in which the covenant with David assumes an importance which in certain respects overshadows even the covenant with Moses at Mt. Sinai (see esp. vs. 11b–16). This chapter closes with a prayer by David in which he accepts these promises made by God through Nathan (vs. 18–29).

It should be remembered here that many OT scholars view this account of Nathan's prophecy as the beginning of the Succession Narrative, that document which describes the dynastic struggles among David's sons to inherit his throne and which, with the exception of 2 Sam 21–24, continues through 1 Kings 2 (see Introduction).

2 Sam 8:1–18 consists of a string of battle reports which read with a telegraphic brevity. The relationship of these various campaigns to one another is not made clear, but if the outline of David's wars of conquest given above is accurate, battles from both phases two and three have been included here. The Moabites (v. 2) and Edomites (vs. 13–14) are both mentioned, as well as the more northerly Aramean kingdoms (vs. 3–12). The fact that the Ammonites are included in the list of David's victims here (v. 12), although the story of their conquest has yet to be told (10:1–19), heightens the impression that a strict chronological precision has not been observed in telling the stories of David's wars. It should be noted that the treatment of the Moabites and Edomites was particularly bloody, and that David's former good relationship with the Moabite ruling family (1 Sam 22:3–4) is now certainly destroyed. Also, the manner in which David treats Rehob's horses (v. 4) was certainly different from that policy Solomon was later to adopt by which horses were held as a valuable resource to be used in commerce. The difference in attitude by the two men toward horses may also signal a more extensive use of chariotry in Solomon's army than in David's.

The final verses of this chapter (15–18) contain a list of David's officials. At least two elements deserve brief mention. The first instance of the use of the name of Zadok, who was to become an important official during Solomon's reign, is registered here (v. 17). His origins are unknown, but some scholars have speculated that he may have been a member of the old Jebusite priesthood of Jerusalem whom David impressed into his own service. Also, the reference to the Cherethites and the Pelethites (v. 18) is doubtless to Philistine mercenaries. Thus, we may see a growing "internationalization" of David's official family.

The account in 9:1–13 of David's kindness to Jonathan's son Mephibosheth (real name: Meribbaal—see 1 Chron 8:34) seems, at first glance, to be an intrusion into the stories of David's wars. In one sense, that may be so, for the narrative is flavored with the same spirit of compassion which was present in the accounts of the David–Jonathan friendship (1 Sam 18:1–5, 20:1–42), and it must originally have been told simply as an example of the fact that David had not forgotten his debt to his old comrade-in-arms (see esp. 1 Sam 20:14–17). Yet, the story may also have another purpose, that of illustrating the manner in which David, at the same time he was fighting his wars of foreign expansion, was also solidifying his loyalties on the "home front." In other words, by bringing Mephibosheth into his own household, he was able to keep an eye on the one person who would be the focus of any pro-Saulite sympathy still in the land.

This longer section comes to a close with an account of David's victorious campaign against the Ammonites and their Aramean allies (10:1–19). The history of David's relationship with the Ammonites has not been preserved, but by virtue of their defeat at the hands of Saul at Jabesh (1 Sam 11:1–15) the rulers of this transjordanian state may have been drawn to David or he to them during David's outlaw days, by virtue of the fact that they shared a common enemy. If such an alliance, not unlike that between David and King Achish of Gath, existed, it would help to explain David's conciliatory move (v. 1), especially if the dead Ammonite king was Saul's old enemy Nahash. The fact that the new king and his counselors suspect David's motives leads to the humiliation of the Hebrew ambassadors and, ultimately, to the wars from which David emerges as victor.

This larger unit, 7:1–10:19, is the final expression of a theological principle which dominates this portion of 1 & 2 Samuel: that is, that God in his grace has chosen David to replace Saul, first by anointing him king, then by working through a complex series of events to place the kingdom in his hands. Beyond this point, the theological mood of the deuteronomistic history will change. Relying on the Succession Narrative, which was composed in the first instance to validate Solomon's right to his father's throne, the deuteronomistic historians will be concerned to describe God's initial steps in fulfilling the promise made to David through Nathan (7:11b–16). And so, theologically conceived, this present unit is both a climax and a transition, as reflected in the structure of 7:8–9 (see 7:18).

For purposes of preaching, the theme of God's grace, being the most decisive theological word in this section, may be dealt with here in a manner similar to the ways suggested for treating this same theme in 1 Sam 16:1–23 and 28:3–31:13. But there are other possibilities also. One could be a sermon (possibly for Mother's or Father's Day) based on 7:14 and entitled "Good Parents Wield Strong Paddles." One hesitates to raise the specter of the corporal punishment of children in a time when child abuse is a matter of national concern (and one should do so, if at all, only in a sensitive manner), but there is a good word to be said for the "old fashioned" axiom about sparing the rod and spoiling the child. 1 Kings 1:6 gives us one of the reasons for the domestic chaos of David's declining years: he was an overly indulgent father. Adonijah was "spoiled," as was perhaps Absalom before him, in the sense that neither son had loving, but carefully defined limits placed upon their behavior by their father. 7:14–15 is referring, of course, not to the behavior of a human parent, but to God's reaction to the behavior of those who were to follow David upon the throne. But the combination of discipline (v. 14) and unwavering love (v. 15) describe well the balance which serves as a model for successful human parenting. I vividly remember when our own children were small that it was usually easier to overlook some act of misbehavior than to go through the trauma of correcting the child. But when a parent follows the easy course, he/she is not always doing the child a favor. The parent is merely making more difficult the next time there is a clash between what the child wants to do and what the parent knows is right. Mother's/Father's Day is not simply a time for honoring our parents, but also a time to remind those of us who are still actively pursuing the parent role that the joys also carry responsibilities. One of the most important of these is the need to discipline our children in

love. They will, in most cases, grow up to love us the more for
our having done that.

Another sermon might be entitled "When We Talk About
God," based on 7:22–23. One of the things the writers of the
Bible rarely if ever engage in is the kind of "God talk" which
describes the Deity in terms of philosophical abstraction.
About the nearest thing to it occurs in such a passage as 7:22
where the biblical writer seems almost at a loss for adequate
words to describe God. So what does he do? He turns to the
specific and the concrete and says, in effect, "If one wishes to
know this great God, one will see evidence of his nature in
what he has done in the life of his people Israel." What a bold
statement that is! It placed Israel in the position of being the
showcase for God's power and love. Needless to say, no one,
not even Israel, was or is able to do that task adequately. And
this is the importance of God's incarnation in Jesus Christ.
God took the fact of his "concreteness" one step farther, so
that in Jesus of Nazareth we see who God is in a unique and
unparalleled manner (John 10:30). And yet, in a sense,
Israel's burden is now the joyous burden of the Christian. In
a world which, if anything, is even less inclined to abstrac-
tions than was the ancient world, when we talk about God,
what our lips profess must be "incarnated" in our lives.

A third sermon theme, this one based on 10:12, might be
entitled "On Being of Good Courage." Joab's words here
come at a time when Israel's battle against the Syrians and
the Ammonites was very much in doubt. Joab's army, in fact,
is threatened with being surrounded and overrun and, although we are given few details, the text suggests that one of
the things which prevents this catastrophe (in addition to his
strategic deployment of troops) is Joab's courageous words.
Here one may wish to compare the words which Shakespeare
puts into the mouth of Henry V (*Henry V*, Act 3, Scene 1
[compare another of the king's speeches in Act 4, Scene 3]).
The point, of course, is not that war should be glorified (one
may be "fighting" for, among other things, an end to the nuclear arms race), but that the presence of courage often deter-
mines the outcome of many of the "battles" of the soul.

The Struggle for the Throne
(2 Samuel 11:1—24:25)

The final major section of 1 & 2 Samuel deals with the unrest which spoiled David's latter years, beginning with the account of David's adultery involving Bathsheba, a narrative which, among other things, serves to illustrate the low level to which human relationships had sunk at the royal court (chaps. 11–12). It then continues by describing the serious threats to David's throne, first by his own son Absalom (chaps. 13–19), and then by the Benjaminite Sheba (chap. 20). As explained in the Introduction, this material was originally a part of the Succession Narrative, which also included the accounts of Adonijah's revolt, Solomon's coronation, and David's death in 1 Kings 1–2, narratives which round out the history of the contest for David's kingdom. The continuity of the Succession Narrative is broken by 2 Sam 21–24, material which the deuteronomistic historians or others inserted from other sources.

David's Sin and Its Consequences (11:1—12:31)

The shocking and forthright quality of 1 Sam 11-12 is difficult to appreciate by the modern reader, saturated as he/she is by tales of violence and sex. In ancient Israel, however, different cultural values prevailed and, although men and women were surely as capable of evil then as now, rarely was that evil described in such detail and in a manner which so exposed the subtle inner workings of the sinner's heart. Moreover, when one remembers that the anti-hero of this incident was none other than King David himself, that "sun" around which the culture and theology of the Jerusalem community was to revolve for almost 400 years (and, in a certain important sense, right up to the present time), it is truly astounding that this tale should have been preserved. Something of its scandalous nature may be gauged by noticing that the Chronicler, who wrote some time during the post-exilic era, passes it by in total silence. Yet the power of this narrative, which lies in its honesty and in its commitment to human justice, is one of the reasons the Bible has lived and is one of the reasons why the faith of ancient Israel is the foundation of three of the world's great religions.

11:1–27 is the account of David's great double sin of adultery and murder. V. 1 serves as a smooth passage of transition which dates the incident to the time of David's Ammonite campaign, recounted in chap. 10. The story itself is as simple in its basic construction as it is complex in its ability to portray the deviousness of David's heart. The king's palace was built on the ridge of Ophel and its resulting height would have afforded David an excellent vantage point from which to look down on the bustling life of the city. Seeing Bathsheba bathing, he is overcome by her beauty and he wickedly relies on his royal prerogatives to indulge his lust (v. 4).

When David learns that Bathsheba is pregnant, he orders home her husband Uriah. David's pretext is to find out how the war is going (v. 7), but his real intention is to arrange for the man to have intercourse with his wife in order that the subsequent birth of the child will raise no suspicions. (If the word "foot" is, as has been suggested, a euphemism for sexual organ [see Ruth 3:4, 7], the command "wash your feet" in v. 8 really means "go home and enjoy your wife.") However, David had not reckoned with the fact that his mischief would be thwarted by Uriah's honesty, for although the man was a Hittite mercenary in David's army, he had no wish to violate the statutes regarding the ritual chastity of the Hebrew fighting man (see 1 Sam 21:4). And so, instead of going home, Uriah simply spends the night in the palace compound (v. 9). Even when David urges him and plies him with alcohol, Uriah will not dishonor himself by having intercourse with his wife (v. 13).

And so, in what may be the most moving part of the story, Uriah is sent back into battle, ignorant of the fact that he is carrying his own death warrant in a sealed communication from David to his general, Joab (vs. 14-15). When David receives the intelligence that his army has suffered a setback before the walls of the Ammonite city of Rabbah, his anger at Joab's foolish tactics (v. 21 suggests that the example of Abimelech [Judg 9:50–57] was a kind of standard military reference in ancient Israel to the effect that one should not

allow his men to venture too near the walls of an enemy forti-
fication) is softened with the realization that Joab arranged
the Hebrew bloodshed as a means of complying with David's
orders (vs. 21-25).

Now that Uriah is dead, David is free to marry Bathsheba. So he adds her to his harem and the son who in due time
is born is claimed as David's own (vs. 26-27).

In 12:1–31 the Lord's denunciation of David is delivered
by Nathan, a man of whom we know little, except that he
was closely attached to the life of David's court (see 1 Kings
1:11–27). From a psychological standpoint, his strategy is
flawless, for he first relates a parable to the king (vs. 1–4)
which is intended to arouse David's sympathies for the oppressed "little man," the kind of figure with whom his own
experiences under Saul would have enabled him to identify.
Only when David's righteous indignation has been properly
kindled (vs. 5–6) does Nathan risk his own life by identifying
the villain as David himself and by drawing the king's attention to the fact that his sin involved something far more serious than a single lamb.

To his credit, David does not banish or kill Nathan, but
rather repents (v. 13), yet not before Nathan (in words some
scholars consider to be a later addition) attributes the coming bloodshed and terror to David's gruesome deed (vs.
10–12). Then, as a further sign of the Lord's displeasure, Nathan, who in an important word of grace has declared that
David's life will be spared (v. 13), looks toward the death of
the infant (v. 14).

The pericope which describes the child's death
(12:15b–23) is in itself a masterpiece of psychological
description. David, who is paralysed with grief over the pros-
pect of the child's death (vs. 16–17), gathers his resources
when the child actually dies and puts grief behind him (vs.
18–23).

The notice of Solomon's birth in vs. 24–25 is an important element in the Succession Narrative, for it is the first
clue as to the outcome of the struggles among David's sons
for the right to possess his throne. Both this description of
Solomon's birth and the preceding account of the death of
his older brother strongly suggest David's deep love for this
wife whom he had won in such a brutal fashion.

Vs. 26–31 finish the story of David's sin by reporting that the Ammonite campaign reaches a victorious climax when David himself, at Joab's invitation, leads the final assault on the city of Rabbah. How ironic that David should enrich himself in this way (vs. 30–31) on the very spot where Uriah and his unnamed companions (11:17) spilled their blood! From a literary standpoint, these verses also bring to a close the account of the Ammonite campaign begun in chap. 10.

This extended section composed of chaps. 11 and 12 is, in addition to being an important statement about God's judgment and love, a brilliant study in the dynamics of human personality. Of the principal characters, only Bathsheba is one dimensional. We know nothing of her feelings or her motivation in this entire episode, since the suggestion occasionally made that her bathing in 11:2 was an effort to seduce David is not supported by the text. It is not until many years later, when the claim to the throne of her son Solomon is being threatened, that she emerges, in so far as our literature is concerned, as a character in her own right (1 Kings 1:15-21).

Uriah, on the other hand, is very much a "flesh and blood" figure whose basic decency, along with the righteousness of Nathan, serves as a foil to the wickedness of the king. Uriah not only demonstrates his faithfulness to the cultic laws of Israel by refusing intercourse with his wife during time of war, but he also shows great commitment to his comrades-in-arms by refusing to claim for himself a pleasure which is denied to his fellows still in the field (11:11—this verse, incidentally, reveals that the practice of carrying the Ark into battle was still in vogue, see 1 Sam 4:3–11). The moment when he returns to the army with the orders for his own execution in hand is the instance of greatest moral outrage in the entire section.

The prophet Nathan is, as noted above, also a man of high principle and great courage. There is a great deal about the office of the court prophet which we do not know, but the temptation to those who served in this office to speak to the king words which he wanted to hear must have been enormous. (See the story of Micaiah and the 400 court prophets in 1 Kings 22.) The nature of the special relationship which was to exist between Nathan and Bathsheba (1 Kings 1:11–21) must have dated from this time.

Of all the characters, of course, that of David is drawn in the boldest strokes. David's sin is multiple: he gives in to his lust, he attempts to manipulate persons and events to "cover" his crime, and, that having failed, he arranges Uriah's murder. The reader of the story cannot help but feel that the judgment rendered on him by God is just (even if 12:10–14 is a later interpolation, it points to the fact that there was a connection between the manner David behaved toward his sons and wives and the troubles that marked his latter years—see 1 Kings 1:6). Yet there is another side to this character, a positive one. Even here, in his darkest moral hour, David recognizes himself when Nathan holds up the "mirror" and he submits himself to the will of God. This is seen not only in his repentance of 12:13 (see Psalm 51), but also in the healthy manner in which he first grieves over the impending death of the unnamed son, then moves beyond grief when the son actually dies. The David of 2 Sam 11 and 12 assumes those complex and forceful qualities which must have been present in the actual person: evil to the point of adultery and murder, yet displaying the power to acknowledge his sin and to accept God's judgment and grace.

This extended passage offers much homiletical material in its rich insights into the heart of man/woman and into the will of God. We might pursue the topic of "The David in Us All." There is a sense in which David is Everyman, because his soul was such a turbulent confluence of the streams of both good and evil. And in the fact there is hope, because God knows us as we are, warts and all. Yet he still wants to claim us and to have us do his work.

Or, as Pogo Possum once reminded us, "We Have Met the Enemy and He is Us." David was an example of many human lives in that the greatest threat to his well-being lay not in external forces (the biblical writers were convinced that God had placed David's enemies in his hands), but in the twisted contours of his own heart. God's grace worked effectively in the life of David and his kingdom, but consider how much heartache and suffering could possibly have been avoided if David's own life and that of his family had been characterized by a higher level of moral integrity. There is a cumulative and corporate sense in which evil works, and one could even argue that the rupture which the nation suffered follow-

ing the death of Solomon (1 Kings 12) had its roots in the
relationships among David's family members. What are the
examples of cumulative and corporate evil around us today?
What seeds of future suffering are we sewing, as individuals
and as a society?

Or one might think about "God's Other Greatest Gift."
On the basis of 1 Cor 13:13 we are accustomed to think that
God's greatest gift is love, and few would wish to quarrel
with Paul's assessment. Yet the prophet Nathan is an example of another gift of God, in some ways as great as the gift of
love. Nathan is a Hebrew word which means "he gave," and
we may consider that Nathan, man of integrity and courage,
is the gift God gave not only to David but to all who over the
years have read and been moved by 2 Sam 11 and 12. The
history of the people of God is punctuated by men and wom-
en who have both possessed moral and spiritual integrity
and who have communicated that integrity to others. History would long ago have come to a dead end if it had not been
for the Nathans whom God has sent. God's other greatest
gift, therefore, may be thought of as that moral toughness
which is rooted firmly in a sense of God's providential concern for all his children. Would that we all possessed this
gift!

Absalom's Rebellion: Its Beginnings (13:1—15:37)

The story of Absalom's revolt forms a long, somewhat
self-contained unit (chs. 13–20). For purposes of this discussion the narrative is divided into three sections, the first, chs.
13–15, being the account of the prelude to the revolt and Absalom's actual call to arms. Observations concerning the use
of this material for preaching have been reserved for the concluding section, 19:1—20:26.

"Evil spawns evil" is a maxim which might characterize
the relationship between David's sinfulness involving Bathsheba and Uriah and the sordid crime which is next reported,
together with the civil disorder that crime prompts. Nathan's words in 12:10 were certainly in the minds of the author of the Succession Narrative and of the deuteronomistic
historians who followed him in placing the account of Absalom's revolt close upon the heels of the story of David's terrible deeds. The king, who had set such a grim personal

example for his wives and his sons, must now witness the harvest of his bitter fruit.

13:1–39 relates Amnon's rape of Tamar. The young woman was, of course, the half-sister of David's eldest son, Amnon, and the full sister of the king's third son, Absalom. (A second son, Chileab [so 3:3, but see 1 Chron 3:1 where he is called Daniel] seems to be dead by the time these events take place.) Love between such close kin was not unknown in OT times, and the fact that Amnon might have claimed Tamar in honorable marriage heightens the tragedy and impulsiveness of his deed (note Tamar's pleading in v. 13).

The story is told with the same frankness and attention to psychological detail which characterize chap. 11 and, indeed, all of the material from the Succession Narrative. The burning lust of Amnon which keeps him awake at night (v. 4), the cunning of Jonadab, and the innocence of Tamar all parade before the eye of the reader in multi-dimensional shapes and forms. And the disgust of Amnon for Tamar (v. 15), once the crime is committed, sharpens the authenticity of the story, as does the narrative's quiet damning of David who, having heard the report of the rape, does nothing (v. 21).

We are not surprised when Absalom takes matters into his own hands (vs. 23–39). The occasion is the annual celebration which follows the end of a successful shearing of the sheep, and the fact that all of the other princes of the realm are present (v. 27) gives to the murder of Amnon the important political implications which become blatantly apparent once Absalom takes up arms against the king. In other words, Absalom seems to have plotted all along not just to avenge the humiliation of his sister, but also to set himself up as next in line to succeed David. It should be remembered that no clear regulations regarding succession to the throne had yet been established in Israel, in light of the fact that Saul and David had both won and kept their thrones by the sword. Thus by resorting to armed insurrection (15:7–12) Absalom was simply doing what his father had done before him and, it will be noted, at the same important place (Hebron).

14:1–33 contains the interesting ruse by which Joab persuades David to recall Absalom from his exile in Geshur, beyond the Jordan, where he had gone to find safety with his

mother's family (13:37; see 3:3). The wise woman of Tekoa
(14:2) apparently enjoyed some reputation in the Bethlehem
area and may, therefore, have already been known to David.
The story that she tells (vs. 5b–7) has certain similarities
with that of Nathan (12:1–4). In both cases a "tall tale" involving human suffering is used as a means of playing upon
David's sympathies, and thus of tricking him into doing
something he might otherwise not have done. Although the
king senses the influence of Joab (v. 19), he allows Absalom
to return home, but will not see him. The account of the extraordinary method by which Absalom, after a period in his
home of two years (it has now been five years since the murder of Amnon), forces Joab to win for him an audience with
the king (vs. 28–33) is preceded by a brief notice of Absalom's
beauty (vs. 25–27).

15:1–37 is the narrative of Absalom's call to arms. The
reasons for his rebellion against David seem to be as stated
above. As the eldest of the royal princes (or certainly the
strongest, if Chileab/Daniel were still alive), he might look
forward to the peaceful accession upon David's death. However, with the method by which royal power was to be transferred very much in doubt, Absalom may have suspected that
David would choose one of his younger, but more favored
sons to become king after him (as actually happened in the
anointing of Solomon during David's lifetime—1 Kings
1:32–37). And so Absalom, upon a pretext (vs. 7–8), goes
secretly to Hebron, the site of David's own coronation by the
elders of Judah (2:4) and the place of Absalom's birth (3:3),
and summons to his side both those who were drawn to his
personal charm (14:25–26) and those who were dissatisfied
with David's rule (15:1–6—notice how Absalom had cleverly
cultivated these people).

David and his close advisers interpret Absalom's move
for what it is and, realizing the large support he has gath-
ered, make plans to leave the city (vs. 13–18). The extent of
the popular feeling against David at this time (and we can
only guess its reasons) is indicated by the fact that those
troops on whom he relies for protection are primarily his
Philistine mercenaries (v. 18). David's long and favorable as-
sociation with the Philistine city of Gath (1 Sam 21:10–15,
27:1–7) is recalled by the passage which portrays the special

loyalty to him of the native of Gath, the commander Ittai (vs. 19–22).

Abiathar and Zadok, David's closest links with the priesthood, accompany the king on his flight (v. 24), bringing with them the Ark of the Covenant. In a remarkable move, David directs that the Ark be returned to the city, commenting that the Lord will judge his cause on its own merits and not on the basis of the presence of that special object in his camp (vs. 25–26). This is one of those instances in which the quality of human freedom, in which the Succession Narrative is so interested (see Introduction), is given expression, for David's action is contrary to much of the religious tradition he had received (see 1 Sam 4:3–4, 2 Sam 11:11).

As the parade of refugees winds up the Mount of Olives, it seems more a funeral procession than a body of soldiers involved in a strategic withdrawal, especially when David receives news that Bathsheba's grandfather (11:3, 23:34) and David's "friend," Ahithopel, has gone over to the rebels (v. 31—possibly because of the king's treatment of the man's granddaughter?). At the top of the Mount, David encounters a certain Hushai, whom he sends back into the city as a spy (vs. 32–37). The tension of the moment is heightened by the notice that Hushai's arrival there coincides with the moment of Absalom's triumphal entry (v. 37).

Absalom's Rebellion: Its Conclusion (16:1–18:33)

The revolt of Absalom, described as a rising storm in chaps. 13–15, now reaches its tragic climax. There are several scenes in this portion of the story, and the author of the Succession Narrative has woven them together with great literary skill and psychological insight.

16:1–23 describes the continuation of David's flight from Jerusalem, begun in 15:13. This was certainly the darkest day in David's life as king, and the humilitaion to his office is sharpened by the manner in which, at the end of the chapter, David is humiliated as a man (vs. 20–22). The events of the day are strung together as beads on a chain and seem intended to heighten the impression that David is an individual who, for the moment, has lost control over his fortunes and is being buffeted by those forces swirling around him. First, Ziba comes to him with the news (which does not ring entire-

ly true in the face of 19:24–30) that Mephibosheth has stayed
in Jerusalem in the hope of receiving his grandfather's
throne (vs. 1–4). Next, David is cursed by a Saulite named
Shimei (vs. 5–14) whom impetuous Joab immediately wants
to kill (v. 9). David's order that the man's life be spared (vs.
10–12) is characterized by unusual restraint and freedom
from traditional ways of reacting to one's enemies. This leniency on David's part may have angered Joab and played
some part in his decision to ignore similar orders by David in
the case of Absalom himself (18:14). Be that as it may, these
two incidents involving Ziba and Shimei indicate that political sympathy for Saul's family was by no means dead.

The chapter concludes with the brief narrative of Absalom's triumphal entry into Jerusalem (vs. 15–23). Vs. 16–19
refer back to 15:37 and prepare the way for Hushai's important role in saving David's life in 17:5–20. The manner in
which Absalom violates David's concubines "in the sight of
all Israel" (vs. 20–23) is an ostentatious signal to the nation
that David has been dishonored and that Absalom is now
king (see comments on the importance of the harem under
2:8–5:5). It is also an important symbol to Absalom's followers that there is now no turning back.

Having proclaimed the political death of David by
means of this sordid act, Absalom now attempts to achieve
David's physical death in 17:1–29. This part of the story is
told in such an ingenious manner that the suspense concerning the fate of the spies is not resolved until the last moment
(v. 21). Just why Absalom would have asked for a second
opinion concerning the best strategy for capturing David
when the advice of Ahithophel was so valued (16:23) is not
clear, but David seems to have suspected that such an opportunity as this might arise when he asked Hushai to be his
agent in the city (15:33–37). Hushai destroys the effect of
Ahithophel's counsel by delivering advice which, if followed,
will allow David time to escape beyond the Jordan. He then
follows this up by sending word to David concerning Absalom's moves by the sons of David's two loyal priests,
Ahimaaz, son of Zadok, and Jonathan, son of Abiathar. The
word is successfully conveyed to David only with the help of
an anonymous maidservant (v. 17) and a certain woman of
Bahurim (vs. 18–20). The aid of these unnamed Israelites

suggests that David had not lost all of his support among the ordinary people.

This story of David's successful escape is concluded when we are told that Ahithophel commits suicide when his advice is rejected (v. 23), that David ends his retreat at Mahanaim, the transjordanian community which was the last stronghold of the dynasty of Saul (vs. 24–26, see 2 Sam 2:8), and that David is offered provisions for himself and his people by three natives of the area, including a certain Barzillai (vs. 27–29).

Had Absalom followed the advise of Ahithophel, David, whose retinue was then in considerable disarray, might easily have been overtaken and killed. But Hushai's clever role has bought the king valuable time in which to find a favorable field of battle. 18:1–33 recounts how David's army, fighting in the nearby (to Mahanaim) Forest of Ephraim, overcomes the forces of Absalom. The ground may have been chosen by Joab because the wooded terrain, where communications would be difficult, would have given his seasoned Hebrew and mercenary troops an advantage over the less experienced militia of Absalom. The story of Absalom's becoming caught in the oak tree is one of the more dramatic moments in the OT (vs. 9–15) and the death of the young man by Joab's hand puts an immediate end to the rebellion. In ignoring David's previous request for leniency (v. 5), Joab was simply acting the good soldier, for he well knew that David's throne would never be secure as long as this hotblooded prince lived.

The information concerning Absalom's burial is followed by a notation about what must have been a wellknown geographical spot, Absalom's monument (vs. 16–18). The information that Absalom had no son is at variance with 14:27.

The interesting story of the manner in which David is given the news of his son's death (vs. 19–33) involves a contest of wills between young Ahimaaz and the "savvy" Joab. Ahimaaz apparently wants to be the first to tell the king the good news out of simple enthusiasm for David's cause. Having recently risked his life to help save the king, he perhaps feels entitled to some such distinction as this. But Joab's preference for the unnamed Cushite (v. 21) probably reflects

his fear that David may react savagely, as he had done in the
cases of those who reported the deaths of Saul (2 Sam 1:15)
and Ishbosheth (2 Sam 4:12). When Ahimaaz thwarts Joab
by means of his own speed and knowledge of the terrain (v.
23), he wisely refrains from telling David the news about Absalom (v. 29), leaving that job to the Cushite, who is also clever enough to speak circumspectly (v. 32). David succumbs to
great anguish, uttering some of the most poignant words in
the OT (v. 33). Fortunately for the Cushite, David is too overcome to be vindictive.

Absalom's Rebellion: Its Effects (19:1–20:26)

Absalom's rebellion has been crushed, but its poisonous
fallout must now be endured. Initially, David's enormous
grief (19:1–8) results in his own paralysis and in the demoral-
ization of those who had risked their lives on his behalf. His
reaction now is at sharp odds with his behavior at the time of
the death of Bathsheba's son (12:16–23), and may suggest a
weakening of his spirit over the intervening years. Whatever
its cause, Joab again acts the soldier and rebukes the king
(vs. 5–7) for his misplaced sympathies and David, to his credit, puts on the best face possible and returns to his duties (v.
8).

As an ominous warning that all of the tensions have not
been drawn from Israel by the successful crushing of the revolt, we are reminded of the bitter rivalry between Judah
and her sister tribes (vs. 9–15). In preparing for his triumphal return to Jerusalem, David foolishly chooses the elders
of Judah, in whose very homeland Absalom had first been
proclaimed king (15:10), to accompany him home and does
so in a way calculated to offend the elders of Israel. To compound his folly, David promises Absalom's commander
Amasa that he will take the place of his own faithful Joab (v.
13—perhaps out of pique at Joab's rebuke of 19:5–7). The climax of this awkward mishandling by David of the relationships among his subjects is recounted (vs. 41–43) in such a
manner as to leave no doubt that the anger of the "men of
Israel" was left to smolder. One wonders what part this incident was to play in their later decision (or that of their descendants) to throw off their allegiance to the dynasty of
David (1 Kings 12).

David's foolish unwillingness to reconcile the differences among the tribes is contrasted and interrupted by three tales of David's gentle treatment of his subjects following the collapse of Absalom's revolt. The Benjaminite Shimei is allowed to live (vs. 16–23) when he begs for mercy (but see 1 Kings 2:8–9, 36–46). Mephibosheth is spared judgment (vs. 24–30) when he protests his loyalty and points an accusing finger at his servant Ziba (v. 26—we come away from this incident not knowing whom to believe, but suspecting that Ziba has tried to capitalize upon an opportunity to advance himself). Finally, Barzillai is offered a rich reward for his help to David during the thick of the rebellion (vs. 31–40, see 17:27), a reward which the old man turns down because of his advanced age.

The revolt of Sheba, which occupies most of 20:1–26, is the occasion for the further settling of old scores washed up by the tide of Absalom's insurrection. The animosity between Judah and her sister tribes seems to be the background of Sheba's defiance of King David (v. 1), a rebellion precipitated by David's cavalier treatment of his non-Judean subjects. The fact that "all the men of Israel withdrew from David" (v. 2) forces the king to turn to his supporters in Judah (v. 4), and is an indication that Sheba's revolt may be considered an early effort to accomplish the same schism which Jeroboam was later to achieve.

Following a brief notice that David put away those concubines whom Absalom had so flagrantly violated (v. 3—they would have been ritually unclean), there is the account of Amasa's death at the hand of Joab (vs. 4–13). There is no reason to believe that Joab would have allowed Amasa to become a permanent threat to his authority any more than he permitted Abner the same distinction, and so a fight between the men was probably inevitable. But the narrative also makes it clear that Amasa was attempting to continue Absalom's revolt. Instead of heading south to mobilize the militia of Judah, as David had instructed (v. 4), he seems to have gone northward, perhaps as an ally of Sheba, but more likely in an effort to foment a rebellion galvanized around his own person. When Amasa does not return to Jerusalem with the warriors of Judah (v. 5), David's regular troops are sent to intercept Sheba. In the process, they come upon Amasa at Gibeon, some 6 miles northwest of Jerusalem, and there Joab

kills him after first pretending to greet him as a friend (vs.
8–10). Initially, Amasa's men seem reluctant to fall in with
the king's regular troops and seem to be paralyzed by the
grisly sight of their leader's corpse. When the body is removed, however, they surge forward to join Joab in pursuit
of the rebellious Sheba (v. 13).

In the meantime, Sheba has taken refuge in a city in the
far north of Israel, Abel-Bethmaacah, near the community of
Dan. After Joab negotiates with a "wise woman" of the town,
he agrees to spare Abel-Bethmaacah in return for Sheba's
head, in view of the city's long tradition of peace and wisdom
within Israel and also in view of the fact that Sheba is all
that Joab is really after (vs. 16–21). When the woman delivers the severed head of the rebel, Joab withdraws his army
and returns home. Not only has the revolt of Sheba ended,
but the long agony of Absalom's rebellion, which began with
the rape of Tamar, has finally concluded, as well.

The chapter ends with a catalog of David's officials (vs.
23–26).

The material in chaps. 13–20, as previously stated, forms
a coherent literary unit. An important piece of the Succession Narrative (see Introduction), it exhibits the theological
outlook of that document and many of the skills of its author.
In this latter category should be placed the manner in which
the stories, as they are told, are constructed so as to claim the
interest and, in some cases, the suspense of the reader. The
author's skill is also betrayed by his/her ability to describe
the "chemistry" by which the human characters interact
with one another, as well as the way in which each individual character is shaped by internal forces of emotion and
intellect.

Because the author of the Succession Narrative was such
a perceptive psychologist and good teller of tales, much of
the homiletical value of this part of 2 Samuel has traditionally been found in its ability to function as a "window" into the
human soul. Here is man/womankind stripped of all of those
masks we love to wear and standing spiritually naked before
the eye of the reader. Here we see not just David and Bathsheba, Joab and Amasa, Absalom, Amnon, and Tamar, but
here we see those who inhabit our own world. Here we see
ourselves! Therefore, the long story of Absalom's revolt offers

rich opportunities for those sermons or parts of sermons which deal with the manner in which human life is lived before God. "The Sins of the Fathers," for example, is illustrated by the manner in which the whole tragic affair which begins in 2 Sam 13 is laid by the author of the this material at the feet of David (cf. 12:10, also note 13:21 and 1 Kings 1:6 as examples of David's permissiveness). In spite of Jer 31:29 and Ezek 18, it is tragically true that the suffering occasioned by an individual's sin is not limited to that individual alone. Or, "Soft of Heart, Soft of Head" could refer to David's inability to come to terms with himself as described in 19:1–8. In other words, genuine grief can easily degenerate into a foolish sentimentality which obscures our true loyalties and damages our friendships. Or, "Five Pounds of Hair" (14:26) might be a reference to young Absalom who was so struck with his own beauty and ability that he allowed his ambition to destroy him.

However, the theological insight of the story of Absalom's rebellion is as important as its psychology. Notice that, whereas the name of God is frequently on the lips of the characters in this drama, as in appeals to inheritance (14:16) in vows (15:7), and in references to places of worship (15:32), only once is God mentioned by our author himself. In 17:14 we are told that Absalom chose the advice of Hushai over that of Ahithophel because "the Lord had ordained it so," in order that "the Lord might bring evil upon Absalom." A single reference, yet what a reference it is, for it remembers David's prayer of 15:31 and says, in effect, that this whole tragic affair concluded as it did because of the will of God. As mentioned in the Introduction, human events seem related to one another in the Succession Narrative in a simple cause and effect manner, without reliance upon the direct intervention of God. Yet here, at this key moment, the grace of God is brought to bear in such a fashion that the outcome of the struggle is decided. Because of Hushai's advice David lives to fight successfully for his life and throne on another day.

This is, of course, a very modern understanding of the relationship between God's presence in our world and the events of our lives, and so we may speak of a "God of the Shadows." Except in unusual circumstances the events of our days can usually be explained in terms of normal cate-

gories of history and personality. To the eye of a given be-
holder, life may be just that and nothing more, "a tale told
by an idiot, full of sound and fury, signifying nothing." Yet
faith in God and discipleship in Jesus Christ involve the
conviction that somewhere just beyond the spectrum of our
sight, somewhere in the shadows, lurks the God of judgment and grace. And in ways which we are better able to
sense than to define he works his loving will upon our history, both corporate and personal. This is the God who is ap-
prehended less by reason than by prayer. And in the final
analysis, this is probably the strongest point the Succession
Narrative wishes to make.

A few suggestions for sermons based on individual texts
within this larger section might include the following:

13:15 will perhaps inspire a sermon entitled "The Good
That I Would."

(1) Amnon's sin was monstrous. In light of his own privi-
    leged position which would have allowed him to
    have his half-sister as his wife (v. 13) his behavior
    was particularly revolting.

(2) Although there are incorrigible persons, to be sure,
    persons who seem to have no flicker of conscience,
    for most wrongdoers there is a frequent revulsion
    over their own evil. Amnon's wish to be rid of Tamar
    (v. 15) may be understood as a strong desire (even if
    Amnon himself did not perceive it as such) to place
    distance between himself and his terrible deed.

(3) This is a turning point in the prince's life. Because
    Amnon did not openly acknowledge his crime and
    seek to make restitution, he brought tragedy upon
    himself, upon Absalom, upon David, and upon all
    Israel. (Compare the destructive nature of Judas' re-
    morse in Matt 27:3–5.)

(4) An interesting contrast to Amnon's reaction to his sin
    is Peter's sensation of guilt as described in Luke
    22:54–62. Peter's ability to face up to his sin and to
    move beyond it by accepting God's grace was an im-
    portant step in his greater service to Christ.

(5) The manner in which we respond to our own evil of-
    ten determines the extent to which we allow God's
    grace to become a reality in our lives. That is why the

confession of sin has always played such an important role in the worship of the people of God. As
Paul's cry in Romans 7:24 reveals, it is not until we
acknowledge our own inadequacy that the forgiving,
strengthening power of God's love breaks through.

Another possible sermon from this section could bear the
title "The Responsibilities of Privilege" and be based on
14:28–33.

(1) A recurrent theme in the Succession Narrative is
David's passivity in the affairs of his kingdom. In this
regard the portrait of the elder David is much different from that of the younger David.

Examples:

13:21: David is angry but does nothing about
Amnon's rape of Tamar.

14:1–21: David admits Absalom back into Jerusalem after Joab's ploy. This is in spite of the fact that
such a step seems against the king's better judgment.

14:28–33: David admits Absalom to court because
of Joab's intercession.

15:1–12: David is passive in the face of Absalom's
obvious assumption of the royal prerogatives (see
esp. vs. 3–4). Compare 1 Kings 6:1.

For the author of the Succession Narrative the troubles which occur during David's latter years are the
result of David's sin (12:11–12) and his weakness.
There may also be an implication within the Succession Narrative that the elder David did not feel a dependence upon God of the same magnitude as the
younger David.

(2) With privilege comes responsibility. When persons
are placed in positions of leadership they often carry
the welfare of others in their hands. No one person
will ever make all the right decisions, but (from the
viewpoint of the Succession Narrative) it is a sin
against God to manage one's responsibilities out of a
spirit of neglect and indolence. Those who have
shaped human events for the better are not those
who have allowed others to make their decisions for
them. Rather, they have acted with strength, resolve,
and (in some cases, at least) prayer and faith in God.

Examples would include Abraham Lincoln, Corrie Ten Boom, and Anwar Sadat.

(3) Most of us will not have responsibilities for armies or the well-being of large numbers of people. Yet in our roles as parents, teachers, businesspersons, or holders of local government office, we must remember that our willingness to stand for principle will effect the lives of others for the better.

A third possible outline could come from 15:19–23: "Greater Love Hath No Man."

(1) These verses describe a remarkable display of loyalty on the part of Ittai and his men, all of them apparently Philistines of Gath. It will be recalled that David had once been in the service of the King of Gath, Achish (1 Sam 27). What connection there may have been between David's service to Achish and Ittai's loyalty is unknown, but this mercenary leader will not leave David's side in spite of the danger. (Compare Ruth's loyalty in another stressful situation— Ruth 1:16–17.)

(2) When others demonstrate loyalty it is important that their trust be reciprocated by means of love and respect. Robert E. Lee's devotion to the men who served faithfully under him is legendary. On the other hand, when loyalty is betrayed, the consequences are tragic. The American Revolution may, in one sense, be seen as the result of loyalty of the colonials (in the early days, at least) betrayed by power brokers in Britain.

(3) The ultimate loyalty and self-giving is that of Christ for the world and the individual men and women in it (John 3:16). The cross is the symbol of this loyalty. How do we respond? In apathy and indifference? In faith and love?

Other sermon possibilities may include the following:

15:24–29: "The Exhilarating Terror of Freedom." We have discussed the insights into the nature of human freedom by the author of the Succession Narrative (see Introduction), and this text is a case in point. David refuses the Ark of the Covenant although the presence of that sacred object with the army in battle has been established by long-standing custom (1 Sam 4:3, 2 Sam 11:11). David is saying, in effect, that God will deal with him on the basis of his own virtues and faults and that he will therefore not attempt to find refuge by hiding behind Israel's most sacred object. The preacher may wish to use this passage to explore the fact that human freedom is both dangerous and wonderful. It is the gift God extends to men and women to enable them to achieve their own potential and to celebrate his presence in their lives through service and love.

18:33–19:8b: "When Priorities Become Scrambled." This text is rich in psychological contrasts and, as noted above, bears some resemblance to 12:1–15 in that Nathan and Joab play similar roles in the two narratives. On the one hand there is David who weeps over his traitorous son, but ignores his soldiers who have risked their lives for him. On the other hand there is Joab who has the courage and the commitment to his own men (see comments above on 15:19–23) to confront the king and to reprimand him for his misplaced priorities. Joab's boldness was not without some danger, as 19:13 reveals (perhaps, as noted earlier, David's final curse upon Joab is also motivated by the commander's rebuke here, although the text [1 Kings 2:5–6, compare 1 Kings 2:32] mentions only his murder of Abner as the cause of his execution). The homiletic value of this passage lies in its ability to demonstrate how our own misplaced loyalties may result in our own unhappiness and in that of those around us. Further evidence of David's frequent inability properly to orient his values may be seen in his rude treatment of the elders of Israel in 19:8c–15, 41–43. (For a posivite example of ordered priorities, see below.)

19:33–40: "When Long Green Is Not Enough." A "cameo" appearance in the drama of David's war with Absalom is made by a certain Barzillai who had helped provision David's army in its flight from Jerusalem (17:27–29), a deed which would have placed him and his family in great jeopardy had Absalom prevailed.

Yet the elderly man is interested in no reward for himself when the triumphant David returns to Jerusalem,
wishing only to be allowed to return to his home in
peace. His action probably does not stem entirely from
the weariness of age (in spite of v. 35), for he seems to
have been energetic enough to respond to David's
emergency. Rather, one suspects that here is a truly
contented person, at peace with himself and with his
neighbors. For him the pomp of life at court held no
attraction, and although he allows (his son?) Chimham
to go with David, he wants no part of the offer for himself. In a world in which far too many persons seem to
be motivated to do things for others only out of hope of
personal reward (Barzillai's world as well as our own),
Barzillai is an exception. His loyalty to David con-
strasts sharply and favorably with David's lack of loyalty in 18:33–19:8b.

Miscellaneous Notices (21:1–22)

The thread of the Succession Narrative is broken for the
moment by the introduction of material from other sources,
an interruption to the "flow" of the story of the struggle for
David's throne which has presumably been made by the
deuteronomistic editors. That story is concluded in 1 Kings
1–2 with the account of Adonijah's revolt, Solomon's accession to the throne, and David's death. Much of the intervening material (2 Sam 21–24), clearly relates to a period early
in David's career, and the reason for its introduction here is a
matter for speculation.

21:1–14 tells the gruesome tale of the execution of seven
of Saul's sons, although there is no report in the OT of the
crime which the citizens of Gibeon allege Saul to have committed against them (v. 1). There is an account in Josh 9 of an
ancient treaty of peace between Gibeon (a non-Hebrew community) and Israel, and Saul may have violated that treaty in
a bloody rampage similar to his treatment of the priests of
Nob (1 Sam 22:6–19). In order to expiate for the crime, David
agrees to the Gibeonites' request for the death of Saul's male
heirs (v. 6), sparing Mephibosheth because of David's "special relationship" with Jonathan. The manner in which
David does this seems to have coincided with some kind of

fertility ritual among the Gibeonites at the time of the barley harvest in the spring. (The Hebrew for "hanged" in v. 9 is unusual and may indicate that the victims were impaled upon stakes.)

The pathetic sight of Rizpah, whose two sons were victims, keeping vigil to protect the corpses from wild birds and beasts (v. 11—the duration of her watch would have been until the fall rains, or almost six months) induces David to take merciful action. Bringing the bodies of Saul and Jonathan (and presumably Saul's other two sons who died with him— 1 Sam 31:2) from Jabesh, he gives to them and to the seven bodies from Gibeon an honorable burial in the family's ground in Benjamin.

The final sentence in the pericope (v. 14b) tells that, in response to this terrible sacrifice God withdrew the famine from the land.

It is impossible to date this incident precisely or to relate it to any other incident during David's career, but the presumption among most scholars is that it occurred early in David's reign. No matter when it may have happened, however, the death of these seven sons of Saul would have been favorable to David's own political designs, for we have already noticed that there was active Saulite sympathy as late as the time of Absalom's revolt (16:5–14). As long as any blood descendant of Saul lived, even Mephibosheth (16:3), there existed an implied threat to David's throne. Therefore, we may have here another instance in which David's own interests are advanced, but are camouflaged as an act of piety and one calculated to advance the common good (see comments under 1:1–2:7).

The theology of this passage is negative. In the light of the love of God which we know in Jesus Christ we may understand that God is not pleased when painful and brutal punishment is inflicted by one person upon another.

21:15–22 is a collection of notices which relate individual acts of heroism on the part of David's men during the Philistine wars. Of special interest is v. 19 which credits the death of Goliath to a certain Bethlehemite named Elhanan. The suggestion has been made that Elhanan is another, "familiar" name for David (his throne name—cf. Solomon/ Jedidiah in 12:24–25). There are problems with that proposal, however, not the least of which is that the name of Elhanan's father is Jaare-oregim, not Jesse.

David's Song of Deliverance (22:1-51)

The hymn in this chapter is almost identical to Psalm 18, with some differences in vocabulary and phraseology. In both places the author is said to be David and the hymn is reported to have been written on an occasion when the Lord saved David "from the hand of all his enemies, and from the hand of Saul" (v. 1). Psalm 18 is the more polished form of the hymn and, although there are also signs of later editorial activity in the Samuel version (e.g., the word "temple" in v. 7), there is no important aspect of the hymn which would prevent one from dating it during the lifetime of David.

There are two major sections of the hymn: vs. 1–31 in which God's power and providence are described (some of the imagery in vs. 8–16 seems very ancient), and vs. 32–51 where, on a more personal level, the king praises God for military and political deliverance. If the hymn does indeed come from David's hand, his profession of innocence in vs. 21–25 seems ironic, perhaps even hypocritical in the light of 2 Sam 11–12. However, if we place its composition in David's outlaw days, as v. 1 tells us to do, that problem is softened somewhat, although his deceit involving the priests of Nob (1 Sam 21:1–5) indicates that he was by no means without guilt even in those early days.

As with many psalms, there is a universality about this hymn which allows it to speak to men and women in a variety of situations. Its imagery is particularly rich in this regard. The metaphors by which God is called "rock," "shield," "stronghold," and the like in vs. 2–4 evoke that strong sense of trust in God which Luther captured in his hymn "A Mighty Fortress" (based, of course, on Psalm 46). The experience of salvation, as captured in vs. 5–7, 17–20, echoes not only the remembrance of the Exodus, but also the Lord's mastery of the waters of chaos at the creation of the world (esp. vs. 5–6, 17). The theophany of vs. 8–16 by which God expresses himself through fire and earthquake recalls the experience of the people at Mt. Sinai (Ex 19:16–24), as well as that of Elijah (1 Kings 19:11–12). If there is any negative theology about which one must exercise care in preaching from this part of the hymn it is to be found is vs. 21-25, words which can be construed so as to support a doctrine of "works righteousness."

In the second section of the psalm, vs. 32-51, many of the same themes are struck as in the first, but here the emphasis is on victory over one's enemies. The concept of God as the Lord of Battle is somewhat out of place in our world where there has been too much terrible suffering inflicted by those who engaged in aggressive warfare because, in part at least, they were convinced that God was on their side. Yet, when we consider that God does have genuine enemies in our time such as war, hunger, economic and political oppression, and an ignorance of his saving ways in Jesus Christ, much of this language of warfare may be claimed for our own purposes by spiritualizing it. (If using the language of warfare to combat the idea of war seems ironic, remember that Wesley, accused of using barroom ballads in services of worship, said that he would sing the songs of Satan himself, if it would advance the cause of the Kingdom of God.) In this regard, the phrase in v. 30, "by thee I can crush a troop," resonates to Paul's affirmation of faith, "I can do all things in him who strengthens me" (Phil 4:13).

More Miscellaneous Notices (23:1-39)

23:1-7 is composed of a hymn which purports to be the "last words of David" (v. 1) and which is similar to the "last words" of Jacob (Gen 49) and Moses (Deut 33). On the basis of style and vocabulary, however, many scholars feel that it is a composition which dates from a time later than that of David. Following an introduction (v. 1), the body of the hymn (vs. 2-5) praises the Davidic monarchy, drawing special attention to the fact that God has established an eternal covenant with David (v. 5). In the theology which was to grow up in Judah around the figure of David this covenant was to rival in importance that established with Moses at Sinai. The final two verses of the hymn (vs. 6-7) address the problem of the wicked (RSV: godless men) in imagery similar to that of Psalm 1.

23:8-39 is composed of a roll of David's mighty warriors. The information is arranged in such a manner as to suggest that David's army was presided over by two orders of military officials. Whether these orders were entirely functional or were partly honorary (compare The Knights of the Garter) is unclear, but ranking seems to have been as follows:

Joab, commander-in-chief (not mentioned in chap. 23)

The Council of the Three
    Josheb-basshebeth (so RSV, but there seems to be
    some textual confusion over his name)
    Eleazar
    Shammah

The Council of the Thirty
    Abishai, Joab's brother, chief of the Thirty
    Benaiah, commander of David's personal guard
    Asahel and the others listed in vs. 24–39.

The number 37 (vs. 39) does not agree with the actual list of warriors in vs. 24–39, and several different suggestions have been advanced to account for this apparent discrepancy. It has been noticed that the list of warriors seems to be chronological, Asahel (vs. 24) being an early follower of David, while Uriah the Hittite (v. 39) was a fighter active during the time of the expansion of David's empire. (It is ironic that the poor man's name should be found here, among David's "heroes.") It has been further pointed out that the list seems to move progressively from Judean, through Israelite, to foreign soldiers of King David.

Of greatest interest with respect to David's life (and therefore with respect to any preaching related to David) is the incident recorded in vs. 13–17, an exploit of the Council of the Three. David refuses to accept their gift of water from the well of his youth on the grounds that he will not satisify his own needs at the expense of the safety and well-being of his men. He instead makes an offering of the water to the Lord. That such an incident would be remembered many years later is an example of the type of dramatic and unexpected gesture by which David won the awe and adoration of those who followed him.

David's Census and Its Consequences (24:1-25)

Chap. 24 is a self-contained literary unit which some scholars view as having originally been a sequel to chap. 21. It contains the remarkable theological view that God incites individuals to perform evil for which he afterwards punishes them. That this view presented difficulties at an early time may be seen by comparing 24:1 to 1 Chron 21:1 where the word "Satan" is substituted for "Lord" (the Chronicler wrote with Samuel-Kings before him, and in most other respects 1 Chron 21 is closely parallel to 2 Sam 24). David's census was considered to be a sinful deed because it moved the monarchy one step nearer to fulfilling all of Samuel's dire warnings recorded in 1 Sam 8:10-18. In this regard, Joab's opposition to the census (v. 3) is worth noting.

From a historical point of view this pericope is of interest because the route taken by Joab and his people (vs. 5-7) is understood to be a description of the borders of Israel at some point during David's reign. Although Joab's circuit includes parts of Phoenicia and Syria, the fact that the census takers did not go as for north as Damascus may indicate that the date of this census is prior to David's campaigns in the far north (see 2 Sam 8:3-12).

David's own conscience convicts him of his sin even before the appearance of the prophet Gad who brings God's word of judgment and three alternative forms of punishment (vs. 10-13). Gad, who is described as both prophet and seer (v. 11), plays much the same role here as that of Nathan in chap. 12. We do not know the relationship between these two spokesmen for God, but the fact that two such outspoken prophets should be attached to the royal court is remarkable. Not knowing which of the terrible alternatives to choose, David casts himself on the mercy of the Lord (v. 14).

The Lord responds with a plague, but it is unclear whether it lasts the full three days promised in v. 13, as the phrase "appointed time" of v. 15 is ambiguous. The impression, however, is that the Lord mercifully cuts short the work of the death angel who, when he is commanded to stop, is standing on the threshing floor of one of the native Jebusite inhabitants of Jerusalem, Araunah.

David, who has been directed by God to build an altar on

this spot where the Lord's mercy prevailed (v. 18, see 1 Sam 6:14), rushes to the spot and is met by a surprised Araunah, who has apparently not seen the angel. The Jebusites' offer of gifts for sacrifice is gratefully declined by David on the grounds that if it is to be his sacrifice, it must be at his personal expense. And so the king buys both the threshing floor and the sacrificial animals and, having built the altar, offers the animals upon it (v. 25). Interestingly, the final statement in v. 25 implies that it was not the act of sacrifice itself which led the Lord to call off the plague, but David's prayers which accompanied the sacrifice (see v. 17).

The statement of the Chronicler in 1 Chron 22:1 which connects the threshing floor of Araunah with the site of the temple is apparently unknown to the original author of 1 Sam 24 and to the deuteronomistic historians who reproduced his material.

As noted above, there are certain problems connected with the theology of this chapter, but at least two positive elements may be noted which should inform our preaching from this passage. The first is that it was not altogether what David did (built an altar, offered sacrifice) that brought about a change in the situation. His attitude also played an important part, and in this respect we may notice some "movement" on David's part. In v. 14 he is indecisive, unable to step between the Lord's wrath and the welfare of his people. But in v. 17 he admits his sin and asks that the punishment be placed where it belongs. The understanding that the posture of the worshipper's heart is of more significance than his/her ritualistic deeds was an important insight of such prophets as Amos (5:21–24) and Hosea (6:6—see Samuel's words in 1 Sam 15:22).

Another positive aspect to the theology of this chapter, one closely tied to the above, is David's attitude toward sacrifice in v. 24. The king rightly understands that one's gifts to God should represent some form of self-denial. To have sacrificed the animals which Araunah offered the king would have made of the whole affair Araunah's, not David's, act of worship. And so David purchases with silver both the site of the sacrifice and the animals. This is the same David, one should remember, who turned the water from the Bethlehem well into a sacrifice to God (23:13–17), the self-denial on that occasion being his own thirst. Perhaps a stewardship sermon could be crafted, based on 24:24, and entitled "Ribbons 'Round the Heart." If colored ribbons are in our time a symbol of gifts (birthday, Christmas, and the like), in theological terms they may also be viewed as those joyful bonds which chain the giver of gifts to him/her who receives. No gift to God *is* a gift unless those cords of joy are also wrapped tightly around our own hearts, that is, around ourselves (see Ps 51:16–17 and, for a more graphic expression of the same theology, Mal 1:13–14).

Bibliography

Students of the Books of Samuel are fortunate to have available a number of fine commentaries. Of these the following should be mentioned: P. Ackroyd, *The First Book of Samuel* and *The Second Book of Samuel* (Cambridge Bible Commentary; Cambridge: Cambridge University, 1971 and 1977, respectively); H. W. Herzberg, *I & II Samuel*, is a translation by J. S. Bowden from the German series, *Das Alte Testament Deutsch* (Old Testment Library; Philadelphia: Westminster, 1964); P. K. McCarter, Jr., *I Samuel* (Anchor Bible; Garden City, N.Y.: Doubleday, 1980), will be followed by a companion volume on Second Samuel; W. McKane, *I and II Samuel* (Torch Commentary Series; London: SCM, 1963) is available in paperback; and J. Mauchline, *1 and 2 Samuel* (New Century Bible Series; London: Oliphants, 1971).

For those who wish to read in some detail of the historical period in which the narratives of the Books of Samuel are set, recommended references would include: J. Bright, *A History of Israel* (3rd ed., Philadelphia: Westminster, 1981), see esp. pp. 179–206; J. H. Hayes and J. M. Miller, eds., *Israelite and Judean History* (Old Testament Library; Philadelphia: Westminster, 1977), pp. 285–363; and M. Noth, *The History of Israel* (2nd ed., New York: Harper and Row, 1960), pp. 141–224.

Interesting discussions of themes related to the Books of Samuel include: A. Alt, *Essays on Old Testament History and Religion* (trans. by R. A. Wilson, Garden City: Doubleday, 1967), pp. 223–309; R.N. Whybray, *The Succession Narrative: A Study of 2 Samuel 9–20 and 1 Kings 1 and 2* (Naperville, Ill.: Allenson, 1968); and the journal *Interpretation*, Vol XXXV, No. 4 (Oct 1981), which devotes its four main articles to a discussion of the Succession Narrative and its interpretation as Scripture.

Pertinent material relating to the literature of the Books of Samuel as well as to the personalities in these books may be found in articles of *The Interpreter's Dictionary of the Bible*. Of special interest are entries on Samuel (S. Szikszai), Saul and David (both by J. M. Myers).

Of interest in its own right is the issue of the manner in which Christians may validly preach from the OT. Helpful discussions may be found in J. Bright, *The Authority of the Old Testment*, an older classic now published in paperback (Grand Rapids: Baker, 1975). A more recent discussion is that of Donald Gowan, *Reclaiming the Old Testament for the Christian Pulpit* (Atlanta: John Knox, 1981). This latter volume gives helpful insights into the manner in which various literary strata in the OT may be dealt with in Christian preaching.

For a more complete list of readings one may consult the bibliography in the commentary by McCarter, pp. 31–44.

The Seattle School
2510 Elliott Ave.
Seattle, WA 98121
theseattleschool.edu